WOODROW WILSON

Woodrow Wilson

A GREAT LIFE IN BRIEF

BY

John A. Garraty

GREENWOOD PRESS, PUBLISHERS
WESTPORT, CONNECTICUT

Library of Congress Cataloging in Publication Data

Garraty, John Arthur, 1920-
  Woodrow Wilson : a great life in brief.

  Reprint of the 1966 issue of the 1956 ed.
published by Knopf, New York, in series: Great
lives in brief.
  Includes index.
  1. Wilson, Woodrow, Pres. U.S., 1856-1924.
2. Presidents--United States--Biography.
E767.G26 1977   973.91'3'0924 [B]   76-54860
ISBN 0-8371-9371-0

© John A. Garraty, 1956

Originally published in 1956 by Alfred A. Knopf, Inc., New York

Reprinted with the permission of Alfred A. Knopf, Inc.

Reprinted in 1977 by Greenwood Press, Inc.

Library of Congress Catalog Card Number   76-54860

ISBN 0-8371-9371-0

Printed in the United States of America

FOR

KATRINE COOLIDGE PERKINS

"Ah, but a man's reach should exceed his grasp,
Or what's a heaven for?"

Robert Browning, *Andrea del Sarto*

PREFACE

I have tried in this biography to tell the story of Wood-row Wilson's life and to portray his character as I see it. But my objective has not been merely to describe. I have also attempted to explain the significance of his career and to discover in his personality some understanding of his actions.

Many people have helped me in this task with their time and wisdom. I must acknowledge particularly my obligations to my wife, Joan Perkins Garraty, and to Walter Adams, Herman Ausubel, Harry J. Brown, Richard M. Dorson, Alfred A. Knopf, Arthur S. Link, Allan Nevins, and Russel Nye. They will all see, upon examining these pages, how extensively I have made use of their many suggestions. I wish here only to express to them my formal thanks, and to point out to other readers that those named are responsible for a large share of what-ever enjoyment and instruction this book may provide.

JOHN A. GARRATY

East Lansing, Michigan
November 7, 1955

WOODROW WILSON

I

ALMOST from the moment Tommy Wilson lisped his first words he had been trained to be perceptive, precise, and accurate. "Steady now, Thomas; wait a minute," his preacher father would caution. "Think! Think what it is you wish to say, and then choose your words to say it." The mind, Joseph Wilson liked to point out, was no "prolix gut to be stuffed" but rather a "digestive" and "assimilating" organ. The boy listened, and learned his lesson well.

And how much else he learned from his handsome, vital father! Throughout his youth, as he developed from fat and placid babyhood into the lean, long-faced youngster who ventured north to attend the College of New Jersey at Princeton, Tommy Wilson found in his father his teacher, his master, his ideal, and his friend. He had been born at Staunton, Virginia, on December 28, 1856, and as far back as he could remember the good Doctor had been the center of his existence. It was his father who took him to visit the cotton gin and the corn mill, who explained the dread meaning of Tommy's earliest memory, the election of the black Republican, Abraham Lincoln, as President of the United States. It was he also who talked with God each evening at family prayers while Tommy, his mother, and his two sisters knelt in reverent meditation, he who presided over happy evenings devoted to reading aloud from "serious" works, but also from Dickens and Sir Walter Scott, and he who, with characteristic intensity, scrambled from his study through the stately house and out into the garden in hot pursuit of his son in a game of tag. "My incomparable

Father," was Tommy's way of epitomizing Doctor Joseph.

The key word in this sentence was "incomparable." Young Tommy strove eagerly to model himself in his progenitor's image. Nature had given him Joseph's quick intelligence, and his sensitive, almost feminine mouth and heavy jaw; he himself must do the rest. But Doctor Wilson established intellectual and moral goals beyond human achievement in his zealous, sensitive son. He unleashed tremendous forces in the boy and set him aflame with ambition, but he thereby left him fated to perpetual dissatisfaction with himself. For who could match such brilliance, such warmth, such stern integrity? Who could meet such uncompromising standards of accuracy and precision, or search so unrelentingly for both knowledge and understanding?

Fortunately, Doctor Wilson also gave his son, in the Presbyterianism of his Scottish ancestors, a strong religious faith that became his "shield and buckler" against all adversity. Tommy Wilson's was the old-fashioned religion of grace before meals, daily Bible-reading, and humble prayer on bended knee. It was a religion beyond argument or reason, in which "all things work together for good." It was the perfect protection against every temptation, the unquestioning resolver of all doubt, a faith beyond petty questions of dogma or history, a "living contact with God," personal and intense. From it came conviction, self-control, determination, and a drive too relentless, perhaps, for a delicate physique. There was a secret understanding between Thomas Woodrow Wilson and his Creator that made him ever a little remote from those with whom he dealt on earth. It was his strength—and his weakness.

However, faith could not completely satisfy self-

doubt. The boy never wholly disguised his basic shyness
and reserve. In many ways he was more like his mother
than his bluff, square-cut father. He had her gray eyes
and plainness of feature, and also her restraint in the presence of strangers, her fervent, almost passionate religious
feelings, and her even, balanced judgment. Like her he
sometimes escaped from his father's hearty vitality into a
world of dreams and lazy contemplation. A Princeton
classmate once quipped that Wilson's first act on taking
up residence was to rush to the library to read Kant's *Cri-
tique of Pure Reason*, and others remarked upon his seri-
ousness and tenacity of purpose, but such friends did not
see him whole. They missed the awkward, uncertain
youth hanging in the background at a party, too conscious of his obligations as a minister's son to join in the
dancing and too ignorant of feminine ways to chat and
banter with the Southern belles at whom he looked so
longingly. They did not comprehend the lonely lad pok-
ing quietly around the Carolina docks dreaming of far-
off places, or the "Mama's boy" with scarcely a friend
outside his own family.

But intellect and will could usually triumph over fear
of personal inadequacy. Tommy Wilson was determined
to become a statesman and he set out early in life to prepare himself. It is fitting that one of his favorite poets,
Wordsworth, composed the line, "the child is father of
the man," for if ever this was true, his was the case. To
be a leader of men one must have a message and be ready
to explain and defend it. Tommy Wilson found his message early in life and readied himself to deliver it with a
single-minded tenacity that was to be characteristic of his
entire career. His intellectual gods were nineteenth-
century Englishmen: Burke, Bagehot, John Bright, and
Gladstone, "the greatest statesman who ever lived." His

political ideal was British parliamentary government—
efficient but historically oriented, responsive to the popular will yet rooted to the past by tradition and a conservative respect for form and custom. His mission was to
awaken America to the virtues of this system.

He was a born organizer. Before he was twelve he had
set up a club in his father's hayloft and written it a constitution. At Princeton he was active in the Whig Society, founded a century earlier by another ambitious undergraduate, James Madison, and he also established the
Liberal Debating Club. (The president of this club was
a figurehead; its prime minister was Wilson.)

One must conceive great ideas, one must organize a
following. But one must also be able to explain, to argue,
to persuade. Oratory was almost as important to Wilson
as his ideals. He had watched his preacher-father practice
the art before countless congregations. Patiently he
worked to master this essential tool of leadership. He studied oratory, and wrote on the subject for the *Prince-
tonian*; during holidays he spouted great speeches by the
hour in his father's empty church. Once a classmate came
upon him in Potter's Woods, declaiming Burke amid the
timber. Gradually he developed a style well fitted to his
earnest nature. He preferred to speak without notes, and
without resort to rhetorical trickery. Argument should
depend on logic buttressed by telling quotations from
the best authorities, not on emotion, apostrophe, gross
gestures, or windy periods. Before he left Princeton he
was a polished speaker and a convincing debater.

Indeed, he seemed well on his way. If he sometimes
appeared to be lazy and an indifferent scholar, the explanation lay in the narrow range and schemeless organization of Princeton's course of study. When challenged,
he could produce work of startling maturity. In his senior

year he wrote an article on "Cabinet Government in the United States," an embryonic development of his political ideas, which was published in Henry Cabot Lodge's *International Review*.

Typically, when it became necessary to cut off some political discussion, he would say with a laugh: "When I meet you in the Senate, I'll argue that out with you." But he was not really jesting. He felt sure that he could "command his own development." Like all youths, he raised his castles in Spain. He even bought a set of blank calling cards and wrote on them in his neat hand: "Thomas Woodrow Wilson, Senator from Virginia." Later in life he denied that in his sophomoric reveries he had ever envisioned becoming President. No higher ambition than the governorship of Virginia had ever been his, he said. And he was perfectly serious.

After Wilson was graduated from Princeton in 1879, he enrolled in the University of Virginia Law School. "The profession I chose was politics; the profession I entered was the law," he explained. "I entered the one because I thought it would lead to the other." But even at Charlottesville most of the formal curriculum did not interest him. He complained of the meaningless technicalities and unrelated masses of facts he was supposed to absorb, and of the pressure placed upon his frail constitution by so much routine. Most of his time he spent in reading history, biography, and poetry, and in improving further his forensic technique. He became president of the Jefferson Society (and immediately began to tinker with its constitution) and wrote articles on John Bright and Gladstone for the university *Magazine*.

Even so, the strain was too much; in the winter of his second year his digestive system began to act up alarmingly, and he had to leave school. There followed a pe-

riod of intense depression and discouragement. "How can
a man with a weak body ever arrive anywhere?" he complained. Back in Wilmington, North Carolina, where
his father was then preaching, he wrote wistful letters to
his university friends, tutored his young brother in Latin,
and tried to continue his studies. In his room he set up a
chart on which he had drawn diagrams illustrating the
gestures he would employ to display various emotions.
He practiced his orations before it by the hour. But solitary study was a poor substitute for college life, which,
despite his complaints, he always enjoyed.

To make matters worse, his first love affair ended
disastrously. While at law school he had fallen in love
with Harriet Woodrow, a cousin living in near-by Staunton. During his enforced idleness after his breakdown he
corresponded with her ardently, but when he visited her
in the summer of 1881 and proposed, she rejected him.
It was after this, perhaps in an effort to start life afresh,
that he dropped his first name and became Woodrow
Wilson.

Although his health gradually improved, Wilson did
not return to Charlottesville; instead he continued his
studies at home. By 1882, although he had no degree,
he felt ready to practice, and after long discussions with
his father determined upon Atlanta as the best place to
begin his career. He settled there in June; and was admitted to the bar in October. By the following May he
had thrown over the law in disgust, a total failure.

A profession as exacting and as full of drudgery as the
law is not likely to reward a cavalier approach. It often is,
as Wilson wished in his case, a means to the end of politics, but the road is usually slow and tedious. Wilson
lacked enough interest in the profession itself to make a
long apprenticeship bearable. It is true that his choice of

location was bad. He settled in a city already overstocked
with legal minds. He had no connections there to throw
business his way. His only real client during his year in
Atlanta was his mother, who put the management of her
small affairs in his hands.

Coming from the cloistered environment of the parson-
age and the college town, he was overwhelmed even by a
backwoods metropolis like Atlanta. He was scandalized
by the city's gross materialism. "Here," he had discovered by 1883, "the chief end of man is certainly to make
money, and money cannot be made except by the most
vulgar methods. The studious man is pronounced impractical and is suspected as a visionary." The pettiness
of everyday legal business discouraged him further—two
talented advocates squabbling over a stolen chicken, the
bitter competition for meaningless cases and insignificant
fees.

And his fellow Atlantans showed no signs of catering
to his political ambitions. He had one brief opportunity.
In January the Tariff Commission held hearings in the
city, and with the help of a young reporter from the New
York *World* named Walter Hines Page, Wilson was
given a chance to testify. He made a strong attack on the
protective system, but the Commissioners were "ill-
natured and sneering" and only a handful of spectators
was present to be influenced by the young lawyer's spirited exhibition of his talents. He tried to follow up this
small advantage by organizing a Free Trade Club, but
aside from giving him another forum from which to practice his oratorical skills it came to nothing.

Frustrated and discouraged, Wilson spent the spring
of 1883 re-examining his prospects. It was easy enough
to rationalize the causes of his failure. "I can never be
happy unless I am enabled to lead an intellectual life," he

explained. Atlanta, bereft of culture, neither understood
nor desired the life of the mind. "The practice of the
law," he continued, "when conducted for purposes of
gain, is antagonistic to the best interests of the intellectual
life." Further, with the growing specialization in careers
and the fierce competition in the profession, a lawyer
could no longer be both lawyer and politician, as was
possible in Webster's day. Now, unless he be dishonest,
a man had to choose one vocation or the other. He could
not be "both a learned lawyer and a profound and public-
spirited statesman."

"My keen desire," he went on, is "to become a master of philosophical discourse, to become capable and apt
in instructing as great a number of persons as possible."
The law, he now believed, did not lead to this end. "My
plain necessity, then, is some profession which will afford
me a moderate support, favorable conditions for study,
and considerable leisure; what better can I be, therefore,
than a professor?"

A year's contact with the rough-and-tumble of the outside world was all that was necessary to drive him back
to the cloister. He would not emerge again for more than
twenty-five years. Indeed, he consciously abandoned the
direct approach to his ultimate ambitions. Soon he was
claiming (evidently forgetting those neatly inscribed calling cards) that "the occupancy of office has never been
an essential part of my political programme," and that he
would be content to remain "an outside force" instead of
a participant in government.

To prepare himself for teaching, Wilson decided to
enter the graduate school at Johns Hopkins. It was a natural choice for a Southerner, for Baltimore, "that beautiful city" with its "grand libraries," would be not too different from Princeton or Charlottesville despite its greater

size. It was also a wise choice, for Hopkins was then the
outstanding graduate school in America, particularly in
Wilson's field of history and political science. Herbert
Baxter Adams's "Historical Seminary" was already famous in 1883 for its sound scholarship and careful imita-
tion of the German "scientific" methods of research. Wilson found himself in a group of brilliant and earnest
students, including Richard T. Ely, the economist, historian J. Franklin Jameson, and Albert Shaw, later editor of
the *Review of Reviews*.

At first he chafed at the formalities of courses and cred-
its, as he had before at Princeton and Virginia. The professors wanted him to work in "institutional history,"
which would involve "digging . . . into the dusty records . . . and other rummaging work of a like dry
kind," whereas he had planned a far broader and more
significant program—"grand excursions amongst imperial
policies," he called it. But after three weeks of work he
managed to bring Adams to his way of thinking. The rest
of his stay at Hopkins was happy and successful. For his
second year he was awarded a highly prized fellowship,
and by the time he left for a teaching position he had
completed *Congressional Government,* a book that won
him an immediate reputation. It was his first taste of real
achievement.

In January 1885 he accepted a position as Associate
in History at the newly organized Bryn Mawr College.
His work was to begin in the fall. In June he married
Ellen Axson.

He had met her in the spring of 1883, when visiting
relatives in Rome, Georgia. Her father was the local
Presbyterian minister, and the young lawyer first noticed
her in church. He was smitten at once. Her shining
golden-brown hair, pink cheeks, and big velvety-brown

eyes turned his mind quickly from the contemplation of heavenly matters to more immediate concerns. Most observers were struck by Ellen Axson's calm sweetness—old photographs show a quiet, soulful face—but to Wilson she seemed a fascinating, exotic creature, a mixture of mischievousness, vitality, and coyness. As soon as he could, he rushed to pay a call on her father.

A rather comic scene ensued, for Dr. Axson was understandably of the opinion that his own charms were responsible for the visit. Only after much desperate conversation-turning was Wilson able to produce in Reverend Axson's mind the brilliant idea of introducing his visitor to Ellen. Then, with Wilson scarcely able to keep his eyes, let alone his mind, off the girl, Reverend Axson blithely forced him into an intricate discussion of the question: Why have night congregations grown so small?

A less determined young man, shy and socially ill at ease as Wilson was, might have given up in the face of such difficulties. But he persisted. After a few more calls even Dr. Axson began to understand his intentions. Wilson's visits to Rome became more frequent. Letters were exchanged; he "could not keep away," must "call every afternoon." There were long walks, picnics, boat rides, drives in the country—a typical Victorian courtship in all its innocent variety.

In September, while Wilson was on his way to Baltimore to begin his studies, he and Ellen met by chance in Asheville, North Carolina. He was between trains. While wandering through the town, he spied her sitting on the porch of a hotel. She had been called home from a visit by her father's illness and was waiting for a train to Rome. He rushed to her side. Picture the two, suddenly together in a strange city, lonely, rather unhappy, each on the verge of an uncertain, rather frightening future. Right there on the hotel porch, Wilson proposed, clinching his argument by quoting his hero Bagehot's opinion that a bachelor was "an amateur in life." Before they went their separate ways they were engaged.

Woodrow Wilson needed a woman in his life more than most men. Only an adoring and adored female could soothe his intensity and provide release from his inhibitions. Despite his complicated nature, Wilson had remarkable self-understanding. He knew he was "sensitive, restless, overwrought." He knew the strength of his passions, and his need for releasing them. "I am carrying a volcano about with me," he once confessed. But he also knew the "sheer impossibility" of confiding in anyone of whose sympathy he "could not be absolutely sure beforehand." Perhaps this constraint was a result of his sheltered childhood, which had kept him almost isolated within the bosom of his family. Or perhaps his early dependence upon the narrow circle of the home was the outcome of a deep-seated reserve. In either case the result was the same. He could never give more than a glimpse of his inner thoughts and affections to an outsider, for to him they were "sacred." "Sacred," he wrote, "not because they are great and rare, but because they are private, personal, not current upon the vulgar tongue." Out on his own in the great world, removed from the sources of his soul's release, he must find refuge in a family of his own. "You are the only person in the world—except for the dear ones at home—" he told Ellen, "with whom I do not have to act a part, to whom I do not have to deal out confidences cautiously." "My salvation," he also confessed, "is in being loved."

Ellen understood her function perfectly and welcomed it; as a result their married life was so idyllic as to appear almost unreal. Not one letter of the hundreds they ex-

changed in thirty years together contains a word of un-
kindness or censure. Ellen's brother, Stockton Axson,
searching his memories in later years; could not find a
single recollection of even a petty family quarrel. To this
harmony each made large contributions. She tolerated his
tenseness and his headstrong, driving ambition. She took
over the management of the family finances and (in the
early days) did without petty luxuries so that he could
have books. She remained at home while he traveled in
search of rest and relaxation they could not both afford.
She edited his manuscripts, kept track of his appointments, guided his steps. He in turn gave her adoration.
After years of marriage he could still write:

. . . if I were *looking* for a poem to express both what I
felt when I first saw you and what all our subsequent life has
shown me of yourself and of the sweet things of love, I
should adopt Wordsworth's "She was a phantom of delight.". . . That poem almost perfectly expresses both my
mind's and my heart's judgments of you.

It is so *dull* to be away from you. Life is so much more *com-
monplace* without you. . . . It is so fresh and sweet and
interesting where you are.

How exciting it is to be writing my last letter before starting
for home! . . . You are the centre of my life, and I seem
to lose force in direct proportion to my distance from you.

Why Wilson accepted a position at Bryn Mawr is not
easy to explain. He could have remained at Hopkins, and
he had at least tentative offers from a number of important
schools. Money first inclined him toward this new
Quaker institution of female education, for he expected
two thousand a year, a good salary for those days. But he
actually received only fifteen hundred, and had to argue

to get that much. In part the very smallness and obscurity of the place appealed to him; he felt that he could learn how to teach there and then move on. Yet when one considers his attitude toward teaching girls, his decision is mystifying.

Wilson had old-fashioned Southern ideas about women. He liked them to be intelligent and educated, but he expected them to obtain their knowledge through some process of osmosis involved in their social relations with highly cultivated men like himself. The idea particularly of working for a woman (and the dean of Bryn Mawr was both female and his own age) was at best disconcerting to him. He felt also that women were "too docile" for a controversial subject like political science. They might do well in literature and languages, but in his field they offered "no intellectual comeback." After he began teaching he complained that the girls even copied his jokes down in their notebooks.

But he needed a job in order to marry, the offer was at hand, and his father urged acceptance. Besides, he would have time to write, and perhaps to do some lecturing in near-by Philadelphia. In any case, September 1885 found young Mr. and Mrs. Wilson settled in a furnished room on the Bryn Mawr campus.

They remained there for three years of hard work, important scholarly accomplishment, children, and much frustration. Ellen studied domestic science in Philadelphia and by their third year had a chance to practice her new knowledge in a home of her own. Woodrow worked on *The State*, his most ambitious scholarly achievement, wrote many articles on political subjects, delivered a series of lectures at Johns Hopkins, and complained mightily about the dullness of female students. All in all they were good years, but when, in the fall of 1888, a call came from Wesleyan with a considerable increase in salary, he did not hesitate. "I have for a long time been hungry for a class of *men*," he wrote a friend. Wilson remained at Wesleyan only two years. He was on his way up in the academic world and moving rapidly. *The State* appeared in 1889; his fame as a lecturer (in and out of the classroom) was spreading. In 1889 he was offered a professorship at Princeton that he could not refuse. He remained at Wesleyan one more year out of a sense of obligation, and he departed with regrets, but he was ready for a broader stage. Wesleyan was delightful, but not sufficiently stimulating. The student body was small, and, he felt, "very inferior in point of preparatory culture." Princeton, old associations aside, would offer proper scope to his talents.

Although it was larger and more important than Wesleyan, Princeton was in 1890 an old-fashioned, small-town, denominational college, quite unlike the great university of today. But it was changing. Powerful forces were at work in the field of higher education, forces typified by the development of graduate study at Johns Hopkins and Charles W. Eliot's reform of the curriculum at Harvard. Princeton, or the College of New Jersey as it was then named, was not immune from these influences. Indeed, the hiring of Wilson was a step—a much larger step than was recognized at the time, of course—in the direction of change and growth.

Wilson represented the new high-powered scholarship. At the same time he was perfectly suited to the role of innovator at Princeton because of his family's impeccably Presbyterian background, his personal dignity and conservatism (he once pointed out that he was frequently mistaken for a man of the cloth), and the strong

support he could muster among the alumni, particularly
with certain influential members of his own class of '79.

These factors, combined with his forcefulness and his
talent for persuasion, soon made him a leader in college
affairs. He helped coach the football team (a choice scrap
of Princeton folklore has him suggesting: "Peradventure
the left tackle would do well to reverse the position of his
feet"), pushed for the adoption of the honor system in
examinations, brought active young men in to staff his
Department of Jurisprudence and Political Economy,
spoke at alumni gatherings, and developed a reputation
as an important and original thinker on educational theory.

He was also phenomenally successful as a teacher.
Comments of students and professors, of friends and foes,
are unanimous on this point. "His lectures were fascinating, and held me spellbound; each was an almost perfect
essay in itself, well rounded and with a distinct literary
style." "I could never stop to take notes." "Every man in
his class felt inspired to do his very best." Professor William Starr Myers writes:

It may be frankly stated here that, after experience with
some very great teachers, I consider Wilson the greatest
class-room lecturer I have ever heard. . . . This is my
mature conviction after experience in my school, college,
and university life.

Even William F. McCombs, who discharged his pent-up
hatred of Wilson in *Making Woodrow Wilson President*, admitted that his lectures "far excelled any courses
given in the University." It is recorded that his classes
were constantly interrupted by spontaneous bursts of applause, and that students unable to register for them

would wait outside the door of his classroom in Dickin-son Hall until five minutes after the beginning of a lecture and then flock in to fill the seats of absentees. And the room held three hundred persons!

Wilson usually began each lecture with a summary of the work to be covered. He would dictate carefully a few general statements or key points, or perhaps offer an outline of the topic in capsule form. Then he would launch into the subject, elaborating, qualifying, illustrating, tempering profundities with flashes of wit, drawing apt comparisons between points he was making and current affairs. He talked from behind his desk, his fingertips balanced on its flat top except when he raised his right hand and pointed at his audience to emphasize a key phrase.

In spite of his success as a lecturer, Wilson was not particularly interested in students and their problems. He concentrated on presenting his material vividly; how well his pupils understood it did not seem to matter much. In the smaller, more advanced classes, which depended more on interpersonal relationships, he was capable but uninspiring. Though the subject was always well organized and lucidly presented, it had no sparkle. In the same way, working with graduate students interested him little. He treated it as a chore, one more drain on his limited strength, not as an opportunity.

In part this was a reflection of his basic nature. He was always far better at reaching large groups than small. Where he could stand as acknowledged leader, where communication flowed only outward from him, he was at his best—and incomparably effective. But it also reflected the degree to which he still looked on teaching as a means to an end. "I constantly feel the disadvantages of the closet," he wrote while at Bryn Mawr. "My ambition is to add something to the statesmanship of the country." At Princeton this ambition was just as strong. Some-times Wilson even resented the "interruptions" in his long-range plans occasioned by his big lecture classes, though his Presbyterian sense of duty always made him apologize when he gave vent to this resentment.

There can be no question of his achievement, how-ever. He was repeatedly voted Princeton's most popular professor—soon he was also her highest-paid. He was deluged with outside offers. The Universities of Illinois, Alabama, Minnesota, Virginia, Nebraska, and Washing-ton all asked for his services as president. But so highly prized was he at Princeton that when further ordinary in-creases in salary became impossible, a small group of wealthy graduates agreed to supplement his income from their private purses in exchange for his promise not to leave. This compact was made in 1898, to run for five years. At the end of the fourth year the problem was solved by Wilson's election as president of Princeton.

A change in leadership had been long in the making. The hiring of Wilson and other forward-looking profes-sors had been only a gesture toward a modernized pro-gram. President Francis L. Patton never fully accepted the new view of higher education. Although a man of wit, charm, and intelligence, he was intensely conserva-tive, a "heresy-hunter" in religious matters, and a foe of all innovations in the college curriculum. When Wilson, for example, had tried to introduce a course in sociology, Patton blocked the change because he feared that soci-ology might undermine the students' respect for divine authority. By 1901 a faculty "revolt" had begun, and the next year the trustees intervened, setting up an executive committee of faculty and trustees that would have ef-fectively bypassed the president and reduced him to the status of a puppet. In the face of this action Patton resigned and, seemingly without preliminary discussion of any kind, the trustees unanimously chose Wilson to succeed him.

It was a tribute to Wilson's achievements that no voice was raised against this precipitate choice. Although he was the first president in the college's history who was not a minister, "every one felt that the right thing had been done." Students, faculty, alumni, and trustees were in complete agreement—a rare thing indeed. And Wilson (who seems to have been as surprised as everyone else) did not hesitate. The presidency was his ticket to the world of action and affairs; it meant an end to a life of "secondary successes." "I feel the weight of the responsibility," he wrote, "but I am glad to say that I do not feel it as a burden." He felt, in fact, "like a new prime minister." The simile is most revealing.

II

WHEN a scholar becomes an administrator, he usually ceases to be a scholar. The press of speech-making, committee work, handshaking, and the thousand and one other duties involved in running a large institution destroys the long periods of quiet so necessary for serious writing, and orients the mind toward the present and the future instead of the past. It is therefore not surprising that the election of Wilson as president of Princeton brought an end to his career as a scholar.

In 1902 Wilson was one of the most prolific and highly regarded political scientists in the nation. Fellow professionals considered him one of the few original thinkers of his generation, and at the same time his less technical works reached a wide public. Even his doctoral dissertation ran through many editions.

The sheer volume of his production was astonishing; in his last ten years as a teacher he brought out nine books and nearly three dozen articles. He accomplished so much, despite an almost constant plague of digestive disorders, headaches, and neuritis, by a rigid regimentation of his time, by systematic organization of his work, and by a tenacity of purpose that at times seemed superhuman. He did most of his work in the mornings in the isolation of his study, guarded by Ellen against interruption. Within this sanctum, crowded though it was with the paraphernalia of scholarship, all was orderliness and efficiency. A book, once used, was not left to clutter the desk; instead it was instantly restored to its proper niche on the shelves. Surrounded by portraits of his gods— Burke, Bagehot, Gladstone, Webster, and his father—

Wilson pored over his notes, and transformed his thoughts into words pecked out carefully on his typewriter.

Once he discussed this method of composition with his colleague Bliss Perry. "When you find yourself at a loss for the right word, don't you light your pipe and walk across the room and perhaps look out of the window?" he asked. When Perry agreed, Wilson retorted: "You lose your concentration. Now I force myself to sit with my fingers on the keys and *make* the right word come." Such was his self-discipline that he could do this, but he paid for it with frequent physical breakdowns.

Wilson's most important book was probably his first, *Congressional Government*. In it he analyzed the operation of the federal system, concluding that, despite the formal separation of powers established in the Constitution, the actual center of authority in the government lay in the House of Representatives, and more particularly in the diverse structure of its committees. Since power was thus diffused and fragmented, it existed without any real responsibility or sound leadership. In the face of this chaotic structure, the President was hardly more than a figurehead, seldom able to institute and carry out policy, despite the dignity and symbolic power lent by his office. In contrast to this, the British government, with its cabinet system centralizing responsibility and power within a small group, provided an ideal structure for a democratic political system.

In recent years it has been fashionable to depreciate the importance and originality of *Congressional Government*. It is true that Wilson was overly influenced by current trends when he wrote off the presidency as being without real power, and that his whole theory was taken over from the well-known analysis of the English system by Walter Bagehot, without even duplicating Bagehot's insight into the real source of power in his own nation—the middle class. Nor did Wilson acknowledge his debt to the *Nation*, which had criticized Congress's committee system as early as 1873, and to others who had formulated his basic idea well before his book appeared. Modern students of government stress the unscientific nature of his approach: his whole argument depends on the *assumption* that diffusion of power confuses the electorate and that a responsible cabinet system dispels such confusion inevitably; he never subjects this assumption to analysis.

But when all this is granted, *Congressional Government* remains an important book. Previous to its appearance American political science had been restricted by a rigid dependence on legal structure. The national government had been studied solely in the light of the formal wording of the Constitution and important commentaries like the Federalist Papers. Wilson, in the words of Edward S. Corwin, was the first to consider the government "from a pragmatic rather than a juristic point of view." And if others had conceived his basic ideas before he did, none save Bagehot had applied them fully and systematically. To say that *Congressional Government* was not as good a book as a classic like Bagehot's *English Constitution* is scarcely criticism. Especially when one recalls that Wilson wrote the book while still at Johns Hopkins, it must be considered a remarkable achievement.

Although the result of much reading and thought, *Congressional Government* was more a work of argument than analysis, more a tract for the times than a scholarly study. This was not true of his next book, *The State*, in which massive research in German, French, and English sources was brought to bear on the problem of the history and development of political institutions. *The State* was a textbook in comparative government; it was also planned as a preparation for a major work to be called "The Philosophy of Politics" which Wilson never got around to writing. Less controversial than his first book, it was a comprehensive and careful treatment of a vast field, and it enjoyed wide and long-continued use as a college text.

Wilson wrote *Congressional Government* while at Hopkins and Bryn Mawr, and *The State* while at Bryn Mawr and Wesleyan. Princeton, which provided Wilson with an ideal setting for scholarly work and where he spent his peak years of professorial productivity, produced no book of comparable quality. He wrote *Division and Reunion*, a brief history of the United States from Jackson's day to 1889, for the "Epochs of America" series, a life of George Washington, two volumes of essays, and, finally, a five-volume *History of the American People*. But all these books were disappointing. Arthur S. Link, after careful analysis, writes:

The more books Wilson wrote . . . the more his scholarship deteriorated. *Division and Reunion* was a careful and scholarly study, written in simple and concise language; but *George Washington* was a popular biography distinguished by nothing except, perhaps, Howard Pyle's illustrations and Wilson's aristocratic affectations and obviously strained literary style. . . . His *History of the American People* . . . apparently served one useful purpose in considerably increasing his income.

Wilson was too much interested in the present to be a good historian. "I will tell you frankly, if you will not let it go further," he once wrote in discussing the *History of the American People*, "that I wrote it, not to instruct any-

body else, but to instruct myself. . . . That may be an
expensive process for other persons who bought the book,
but I lived in the United States and my interest in learning their history was, not to remember what happened,
but to find which way we were going."

Thus, when Wilson became president of Princeton,
the scholarly world suffered no tragic loss. In spite of his
large output and his ability to concentrate completely on
literary tasks, he had never been ready to devote his
whole life to academic study. He talked about how
"heartbreaking" it would be to have to give up writing
even temporarily, but also pointed out that "duty," a
"singularly plain, a blessedly plain" case of "duty," made
the switch necessary. Actually, as Bliss Perry once remarked, Wilson "romanticized 'affairs' . . . the practical business of the world," and seized eagerly the opportunity to take part in them.

College presidents are commonly known as "educa-
tors," but in most cases they function more as publicity
men and professional fund-raisers than as trainers of the
youthful mind. Wilson, however, was really an educator.
His goal was to make Princeton a great university by
broadening the scope of its courses, improving the quality
of the teaching staff, and raising the academic standards
of the students. He sought to do all this not as an end in
itself, not because of any love of knowledge for its own
sake, but because he felt that the modern world urgently
required the kinds of services that university-educated
persons could provide. "It is plain what the nation needs
as its affairs grow more and more complex," he said in
his stirring inaugural. "It needs efficient and enlightened
men. The universities of the country must take part in
supplying them."

At first Wilson achieved remarkable success with his

plans. He had the great advantage of knowing exactly what he wanted to do, and his position was strengthened by the unswerving support of the trustees, who were inspired by his vision and eager to give a new man every possible benefit. In his first report he asked for twelve million dollars of new endowment (the total endowment at that time was only four million) to cover his plans for new staff and buildings—in short, to "create a real university."

All of this was not, of course, forthcoming. Wilson himself did little to raise funds aside from "inspiring" the trustees to do so. He did little because he was too thin-skinned to go a-begging among the well-heeled alumni in search of money. "Woodrow was no earthly good at it," a niece recalled in discussing this aspect of his nature. He could sit down and write: "I have set forth the most immediate needs of the University in the report to the Board of Trustees, which I take the liberty of sending you . . . ," but when it came to collaring the big potential donors he was useless. In the long run it was money—both the need of it and its very availability— that was to prove his undoing at Princeton.

The first, least controversial, and probably most significant step Wilson took was a revision of the curriculum. The traditional nineteenth-century college curriculum had been narrowly classical and rigidly organized. In the seventies Charles W. Eliot had instituted a revolution at Harvard by setting up a program of wide coverage and free choice, commonly called the elective system. Wilson steered between these extremes. Many new courses were added, but the emphasis was on logical organization. Freshman students had no choice of courses, and sophomores very little. Upperclassmen could select, but only from "a scheme of related subjects." The result, providing a flexibility absent in the old system without the chaos of the Harvard plan, was all that Wilson had hoped for, and in time even Harvard came to see its virtues.

But it was not enough to provide the student with an integrated education; he must also be made to absorb it. This required a raising of standards. Before Wilson took office Princeton had been something of a finishing school for young gentlemen. This the new president determined to change. Entrance requirements were stiffened, and in the process a number of boys of high moral and social standing but low academic records were turned away. This led to trouble, but Wilson faced it inflexibly. When someone complained of such a case, Wilson replied coldly: "Pardon me, you do not understand. He did not pass the entrance examinations. . . . If the angel Gabriel applied for admission to Princeton University and could not pass the entrance examinations, he would not be admitted."

This policy resulted in a temporary decline in enrollment, and there was a good deal of student grumbling. One disillusioned youngster is said to have written his father: "Princeton is getting to be nothing but a damned educational institution." The *Tiger* published a cartoon showing a cap-and-gowned Wilson seated forlornly on the steps of a deserted Nassau Hall. Below it was this caption, taken from the well-known whisky advertisement: "Wilson—That's All." But the new standards were maintained, and the student body was forced to adapt itself to them. In the long run everyone benefited.

In addition to improving courses and standards, Wilson also undertook to improve the teaching methods used at Princeton. Here too he achieved success, although of a less permanent kind.

It is strange, considering his own experiences as a teacher, that Wilson espoused the tutorial system so vigorously. He had had his great success as a lecturer before large audiences, yet in December 1902 he told an alumni group that only in small classes, where the students "can be intimately associated with their chief," could real learning take place. This was to be accomplished not by abandoning the lecture system, but by hiring fifty new faculty members, to be called preceptors, who, operating within the departments, would guide the development and reading of all upperclassmen.

For a school the size of Princeton, the hiring of fifty instructors was a titanic undertaking. In dollars alone it involved a formidable sum; in terms of obtaining that many new teachers of real quality, the problem was even greater. Yet Wilson accomplished it. He was not able to find the necessary endowment (though he forced himself to try), but by appealing to the alumni through speeches at dinners, where he was at his incomparable best, he accumulated enough money to run the program for three years. The preceptors themselves he obtained through the sheer force of his personality and his magnificent enthusiasm.

One by one he called the best young men he could find to Princeton for interviews. Professor Robert K. Root recalled his own experience thus:

My interview lasted some forty minutes. Mr. Wilson asked me no questions about myself, but spoke with winning eloquence about his plans for Princeton. Before five minutes had passed I knew that I was in the presence of a very great man. . . . I had never before talked face to face with so compelling a person. Before the talk was over my loyalties were entirely committed to him. Had Woodrow Wilson asked me to go with him . . . while he inaugurated a new

university in Kamchatka or Senegambia I would have said
"yes" without further question.

Others reacted in much the same way. "What brought
you to Princeton?" one new faculty member asked bi-
ologist Edward G. Conklin. "Woodrow Wilson," he
replied. "And you?" "The same," his colleague admitted.

The tutorial system was stimulating for student and
teacher alike, but it involved certain impracticalities
which in time forced modifications of its structure. Aside
from its great cost, it placed a tremendous burden of work
on the preceptors. Professor Edward S. Corwin estimated
that he taught between sixteen and seventeen hours per
week under the program, and in addition had to read between ten and twenty thousand pages a year in preparation for the discussions he led. Wilson's reorganization of
the curriculum had integrated related subjects into large
departments; each tutor had to direct work in one of these
wide fields. Corwin, for instance, was a member of the
Department of History, Politics, and Economics, and
had to keep up with all three areas of knowledge. Wilson's infectious enthusiasm could carry only so far. In
time the tutors began to complain of overwork and of the
fact that they were denied the opportunity to teach spe-
cialized courses of their own. And so changes had to be
made, though the tutorial method continues to be used
at Princeton today.

The preceptors first appeared on the Princeton campus
in the autumn of 1905. By the end of that academic year
the virtues of the system had been proved, and Wilson
was at the height of his popularity and power. The campus seemed alive with a new spirit, students buckling
down to work, young professors pedaling furiously from

one building to another to meet their classes, visiting alumni beaming proudly in the reflected glory of the school's achievements. "Wilson is Princeton's most valuable asset," became a local slogan. The trustees themselves acknowledged his leadership. They consulted him at every step, found the money he continually demanded, and even purged their own body of dissidents.

Had Wilson been content to slow the pace of his reforms at this point, he would probably have passed the rest of his life peacefully at Princeton. But he was brimful of additional ideas; his successes only stirred him to more daring endeavors. In 1907 he introduced his quadrangle plan for further integrating the life of the students, an event that marked the beginning of his fall from power.

The proposal, briefly, was this: The entire student body was to be divided into groups which would live together in largely self-governing sub-communities called quadrangles. These groups would cut across academic class lines; lowerclassmen, upperclassmen, and unmarried members of the faculty would sleep, eat, and study together in a single plant. Freshmen and sophomores would gain much from association with the older boys, and to these, in turn, the presence of faculty members would be but an extension of the preceptorial idea. All would benefit from close co-operation in the interest of learning—"education would become a life process." "We have tutor and pupil," Wilson reasoned. "Now we must have pupil and pupil in a comradeship of studies."

At a board meeting on June 10, 1907, Wilson presented the scheme formally to the trustees, who approved it in principle with only one dissenting vote. But when its nature became known, strong opposition developed among the faculty and alumni. There already existed at Princeton a number of upperclass eating clubs to which at least two thirds of the juniors and seniors belonged. The quadrangle plan would mean their destruction.

These clubs were rich and powerful organizations. Membership involved a certain cachet which ambitious and socially prominent students sought eagerly. Club men developed strong loyalties to "Tiger Inn, "Cap and Gown," "Ivy," and the others—loyalties which persisted beyond graduation and stirred the hearts of many influential alumni when their clubs were attacked. Soon such men were showering the campus with criticism of a plan they felt would undermine college traditions and destroy school spirit. They were supported by some of the older members of the faculty, who resented the fact that Wilson had not consulted them in advance, and by certain practical-minded souls who were disturbed by the probable cost of constructing the quadrangles and the president's blissful lack of interest in the details of what was bound to be a very complex alteration of the structure of Princeton. Throughout the summer of 1907 a bitter controversy raged.

Much could be said on both sides of the question. No one denied that the clubs were well run, orderly, and an ornament to the social side of college life. They served a useful function in feeding a large segment of the undergraduate population, and provided an environment in which many lasting friendships were made. On the other hand, they were decidedly anti-intellectual in spirit, and had assumed an importance in the student mind out of proportion to their merits. They were also exclusive. Many boys did not "make" a club, and some suffered serious emotional damage. Both their anti-intellectual and anti-democratic aspects influenced Wilson's decision to abolish the clubs, but he placed his chief stress on the first of these failings.

He was able to carry a solid majority of the faculty with him, but an equally clear majority of the alumni dissented. Thus the trustees were faced with a serious problem. True, it was one of their own making. Wilson had explained his intentions fully when he presented the plan. But undoubtedly some trustees had gone along without considering all the plan's implications, chiefly out of admiration for Wilson's past achievements, and others without realizing that when they had authorized him "to take such steps as may seem wisest for maturing this general plan" he would insist on forcing it through at once. Further thought led several to change their minds, and even some of his strongest supporters on the board began to urge that he slow down. Principles aside, many trustees were becoming alarmed at the state of the university's finances. With the preceptorial system operating from hand to mouth, the expensive building program needed to provide plant for the quadrangles seemed out of the question. At the October board meeting, therefore, the trustees reversed their approval of the plan.

Wilson was crushed. "I thought that they meant what they said when they offered to leave me free," he complained bitterly. For a time he considered resigning, but feared that might "place the University in danger of going to pieces"; then he sought divine guidance to discover "what my duty is now." Finally he fought back, appealing to alumni groups in a series of impassioned speeches. But it was useless. A crippling attack of neuritis, as much mental as physical in origin, forced him to drop the struggle. In April 1908 the trustees, gently but firmly, more in sorrow than in anger, wrote a quietus to the quadrangle plan by formally declaring their support of the club system.

Wilson's reputation emerged from the quadrangle fight

somewhat scarred but essentially intact. While he had made a few implacable enemies and lost (entirely through his own choosing) a few close friends, he still held the confidence of a majority of all those concerned with Princeton's welfare. The real significance of the affair is that it reveals his typical response to opposition.

He had always been determined, forceful, intellectually self-confident. He had always been contemptuous of stupidity, impatient with dull formalities and narrow opportunism alike. His belief in his own rectitude, based in part on his awareness of his superb mental equipment and in part on his unshakable religious faith, was well developed long before he became president of Princeton. "A Scotch-Irishman," he frequently remarked, *"knows* that he is right." Power, with its concomitant success, reinforced all these aspects of his character. These qualities were largely responsible for his effectiveness as a leader, but they also contributed to his defeat in the quadrangle fight.

Wilson's motives in introducing the plan were unexceptionable. His mistake lay in his refusal to accept less than the whole thing, in his tactless handling of those who opposed him, and in his determination, as he put it in discussing another matter with Bliss Perry, to *"see who is master"* once the conflict had broken out.

Yet it was not in him to do other than he did. If he had been willing to compromise, he could have converted the clubs into something very close to what he wanted the quadrangles to be. If he had been better at understanding people, he would not have insinuated that trustee Moses Taylor Pyne, a man whose selfless devotion to Princeton was legendary, was "dominated by the club men," merely because he had reversed his position. If he had been less demanding in his friendships, he would not have been cut to the quick when his closest Princeton friend, Professor John G. Hibben, seeking "to save Woodrow from himself," opposed the quadrangle plan in faculty meeting. The quadrangle battle proved that Wilson was a formidable fighter, but also an inflexible one.

The clash over the eating clubs aggravated another Princeton problem that had been building up over the years. This concerned the expansion of the graduate school. The club controversy had been largely impersonal; it arrayed groups against one another more than individuals. But the graduate-school controversy was chiefly a battle between two men, Wilson and Andrew Fleming West. Superficially they had much in common. Both were sons of Presbyterian ministers, both Princetonians, both first-rate scholars who had taken the lead in the nineties in the fight to modernize their alma mater. Both had, after 1896, devoted more and more time to administration and less and less to scholarship.

Yet underneath they were entirely different. West was bluff, hearty, hail-fellow-well-met. A hulking man (he weighed well over two hundred pounds), he was at his best in close personal relationships of the kind that Wilson could not handle. He had a way with the old grads, particularly with those possessed of large sums of loose cash that might somehow be transferred to Princeton's coffers. He could spot a potential donor on the campus, accost him with a warm greeting and a friendly hand on the shoulder, "giving the impression that he had been longing for weeks to run across just this particular fellow." It was quite natural that he should be an intimate of Princeton's most distinguished trustee, ex-President Grover Cleveland, a man much like himself.

When Wilson became president of Princeton, West

was dean of the graduate school, devoting all his fierce loyalties and extraordinary energies to its advancement. That summer, with $2,500 provided by the trustees, he visited the leading European universities to study their methods of housing graduate students. He returned deeply impressed, especially by Oxford, where he had been awarded an honorary LL.D., and wrote an elaborate report describing his plans to construct a new graduate school, the "crown" of Princeton's educational system. Wilson, to his great chagrin later on, provided this report with a preface in which he said: "the plans . . . which Professor West has conceived seem to me in every way admirable."

In the controversy that developed, the ostensible cause of the trouble between Wilson and West was the *location* of the graduate school. West wished to build it off by itself, secluded from the distractions of undergraduate life, while Wilson, with his passion for integration, wanted it in the heart of the campus. Actually, the real cause was personal. Wilson had never liked West, whom he considered bigoted and conspiratorial. Furthermore, while supporting its development in principle, Wilson was less interested in the graduate school than in his own multifarious projects. And he resented West's power, which had increased greatly during the "do-nothing" Patton regime.

Whatever the justification for Wilson's attitude, he should have forced a showdown with West early in his administration. He had a perfect opportunity to do so in 1906, when West was offered the presidency of M.I.T. at a handsome salary. West, who well understood Wilson's feelings, was ready to make the move. At a dramatic meeting of the trustees' committee on the graduate school, he told Wilson plainly that he would not continue at Princeton unless he could have his own way in working out the graduate program. "The trouble, President Wilson," he stated frankly, "is that I have not hit it off with you."

But at this juncture Wilson exhibited one of his most curious failings. He hated to base a decision on personal feelings; he could not face West's departure on such an issue. He therefore joined with the trustees in asking West to remain, stressing that "the Board has particularly counted upon him" for the developing of the graduate school.

West, with his great affection for Princeton, accepted this as meeting his demands, and gave up the M.I.T. position. His anger when Wilson began to push the quadrangle plan a few months later was understandable. Princeton was already short of funds. It seemed clear that the quads and the graduate school could not be built at the same time, and that the graduate school would be sidetracked. As though this were not enough, Wilson then persuaded the trustees to transfer most of the dean's power to a faculty committee dominated by Wilson's supporters. When West protested this injustice, Wilson coolly remarked: "I wish to say to the Dean, somewhat grimly, that he must be digested in the processes of the University," and when West brought up the promises made him in 1906, Wilson answered: "We must not lay too great stress on commitments."

This conference took place on February 5, 1909. A lesser man might have been crushed, but West struck back. One of his closest friends was William C. Procter, head of Procter and Gamble and a devoted Princeton alumnus. West explained the nature of his problems to Procter. Procter was sympathetic. In May, West was able to announce that the maker of Ivory Soap had of-

fered Princeton half a million dollars to build a graduate
college. There was but one stipulation. Procter had visited the campus, "examined" the site that Wilson had
picked for the building, and found it "not suitable." Unless a different location was found, the offer would be
withdrawn.

In the following uproar everyone involved seems to
have lost his grip on reality. Obviously Procter's proviso
was inspired by West. The dean had good reason to be
angry with Wilson, but his action was hardly in keeping
with his responsibilities to Princeton. Wilson, for his part,
could and did take the sound position that donors should
not be allowed to control university policy. He urged the
trustees to refuse the offer. But this particular case was
scarcely important enough to make an issue of. Soon the
trustees, the faculty, and the alumni were split wide
open—over the "momentous" question: Should the
graduate school be here, or here?

The battle raged furiously for more than a year, the
actions of the principals growing more and more discreditable. The trustees voted to accept the money and
Wilson threatened to resign. The trustees then prepared
to reverse themselves and Procter countered by withdrawing his offer. In the meantime Wilson appealed to
the alumni in a series of unrestrained speeches in which
he sought to identify an "integrated" graduate school
with democracy and a "separated" one with aristocracy.
Tempers flared among the trustees as Wilson shifted his
ground, tangling himself in inconsistencies and plain lies.
At one hot committee meeting he stated the truth: that
the real issue was his own disagreement with West. The
site, he admitted, was unimportant; "my faculty can
make this school a success anywhere in Mercer County."
When a hostile trustee pounced upon this and asked him

why then he had written his fulsome praise of West's plan in his preface to the dean's report, he announced that he had not seen the report at the time he wrote the preface! This was an outright falsehood, for he had read and revised West's manuscript.

It was this mutual antagonism and mistrust that made Wilson's resignation inevitable, although the final blow came from a totally unexpected quarter. On May 22, 1910 Wilson received a telegram. A few minutes later his wife heard him laughing in his study. She found him holding the yellow slip in his hand. "We have beaten the living," he said, "but we cannot fight the dead. The game is up."

The telegram was from Dean West. Isaac C. Wyman of Salem, Massachusetts, had just passed away. He had left his estate, "at least two millions and may be more," to Princeton's graduate school. He had named as his executor—Andrew Fleming West.

Commencement a few weeks later was devoted to the glorification of Wilson's enemies. The air about the president was hostile. The victors waited with patience but determination for him to step aside. Before the October meeting of the board a delegation called upon him to tell him that he must step down. Next day he faced the trustees, read his brief note of resignation, and left the meeting. There was neither discussion nor comment. The trustees then voted to accept his resignation, with, they said, "deep regret." His former friend John G. Hibben was chosen to replace him.

It made a sad and ugly end to twenty years of his life. Fortunately, however, a new demand for his services had arisen. Already, as he left the trustees' meeting, he was the Democratic candidate for governor of New Jersey. A new career was to rise from the ashes of the old.

III

WOODROW WILSON, architect of the New Freedom and idol of a generation of liberals, was given his great political opportunity because he was a conservative. The man who was to push more reform legislation through Congress than any previous president was first recommended to the nation's voters by a business associate of J. P. Morgan; the man who was to declare war on machine politics was elected governor of New Jersey chiefly through the efforts of one of the most notorious bosses in the state's history.

These supporters did not misunderstand Woodrow Wilson. He, rather, misunderstood himself. For despite his reverence for the world of "affairs" and his lifelong ambition for political office, he was terribly naïve about the political and economic realities of his own times. His conservative backers, by making possible his "education," destroyed the Wilson they knew and liked and created another Wilson they never could understand and were soon to despise.

In their disillusionment they were to call him a trimmer, an opportunist, a monstrous unprincipled fraud. They would have agreed with Wilson's great enemy, the arch-Republican senator from Massachusetts, Henry Cabot Lodge, who said on the eve of Wilson's election as president: "A man can change one or two of his opinions for his own advantage and change them perfectly honestly, but when a man changes all the well considered opinions of a life time and changes them all at once . . . it seems to me that he must lack in loyalty of conviction." But they, like Lodge, would have been

wrong. Wilson changed his mind, and his political fortunes prospered accordingly. Though it would be foolish
to deny that practical politics made the change easier, the
change was patently sincere. If it was quick, it was because his awakening had been sudden and because his
mind, once alerted to a new concept, always engulfed
and assimilated it with startling swiftness.

When a young man, Wilson had never been a conscious defender of reaction and special privilege, but as
an ardent disciple of Burke he was intellectually committed to conservatism. Though a Virginia Democrat, he
was no great admirer of Jefferson, who, he said, had
been too much influenced by the radicalism of the French
Revolution. While at the University of Virginia, where
Jefferson was revered almost as a god, he considered himself "somewhat of a Federalist," and never even bothered
to climb the hill to visit Monticello. In the dark Atlanta
period, he was appalled by the radicalism of the Georgia
legislature, which had passed resolutions in support of
federal aid to education. "I heard but one speech in opposition to this begging resolution," the young lawyer
had written a college friend indignantly. "The whole
proceeding impressed me as a shameless declaration of
the determination of a well-to-do community, to enjoy the
easy position of a beneficiary of the national govt. to the
fullest possible extent."

All his scholarly writings reflected distrust, if not dislike, of democracy. Both his background as a Southern
"aristocrat" and his arrogance as a university "intellectual" caused him to minimize the capacities of the common man; the cloistered life was poor training for one so
unversed in practical economics. Throughout the troubled nineties he remained oblivious to the injustices which
stirred so many breasts and which gave birth to Populism

and the career of William Jennings Bryan. He laughed at the emotionalism of Bryan's "Cross of Gold" speech at the 1896 Democratic convention, and refused to vote for him in the election.

As late as 1907 he maintained that the burgeoning industrial monopolies were both necessary and desirable, and that labor unions were un-American, since they deprived the worker of the right to dispose of his labor in any way he saw fit. Anti-social activities by business should be checked by punishing individual violators under existing civil and criminal law, not by breaking up trusts or imposing large fines on corporations. He called for the creation of a "people's forum" to take the lead in formulating policy for the nation, and suggested that the mighty banker, J. P. Morgan, would be an ideal chairman for such a group.

All these views naturally endeared him to the conservative elements in the nation. These groups, under attack during the first decade of the century from both Democrats like Bryan and Republicans like Roosevelt, approved of his economic and political doctrines and also his high moral tone. Such a man, they felt, could (without undermining the basic structure of a society they found, on the whole, eminently satisfactory) root out the thieves and cheats who threatened to destroy business ethics. He could give them moderate change by means of conservative reforms patterned on the constitution and on historical precedent.

When, having been given his chance by these conservatives, Wilson proceeded to reverse himself almost completely, his benefactors were most bitter. Actually, if they had followed his development closely and impartially instead of seizing upon those words and phrases in his pronouncements that they found reassuring, they

would have noted a gradual shift in his thinking throughout the years of his presidency of Princeton. Although
he continued critical of Bryan, by 1904 he was coming
to accept Bryan's aims as essentially sound. Except that
the Nebraskan lacked a "mental rudder," Wilson told a
friend, he might make a fine leader. Within the next year
or two Wilson became increasingly aware of the economic and social problems faced by the United States as
a result of rapid industrialization. But for his deep theo-
retical commitments to Manchester economics and to
Edmund Burke's brand of political conservatism, he
would probably have moved to a progressive position far
more rapidly than he did.

As it was, he moved gradually from the right at least
in the direction of the center. In 1906, in an address before the Democratic Club of New York, he spoke flat-
teringly (if somewhat vaguely) about Jefferson. The
next year, in a series of lectures at Columbia University,
he revised drastically his view of the role of the president
in national politics. Instead of the empty figurehead described in *Congressional Government*, the chief executive now seemed to him the only national voice in "affairs." In the hands of a real leader, the office could be
an instrument for the perfection of democracy, a means
for centering responsibility and giving voice to the will of
the people.

By 1908 the shift in Wilson's thinking had become
more noticeable. It is difficult to pinpoint the time when
he crossed the watershed between conservatism and lib-
eralism, but a meeting of the Princeton Politics Club in
the home of Professor Paul van Dyke may well have
been the moment. The date was May 8, 1908. Some
twenty academicians were discussing Theodore Roosevelt's career as president. Wilson led the attack on T.R.;

he denounced his cavalier approach to the Constitution, his stress on big government, and his overbearing use of personal power in bending Congress and the Departments to his will. There was nothing liberal in what Wilson said, but when some of his colleagues, led by Professors Corwin and Garfield, defended Roosevelt spiritedly, he seemed pleased with their speeches, almost as though he had taken the other side to draw them out and test his own ideas. Years later, he remarked ruefully that young Corwin had "wiped the floor" with him in the discussion.

In any case, his public utterances shortly took on a more liberal tone. He began to use the phrase "privileged interests" in unfavorable contrast with "general interests" and spoke of "restraining" the former to protect the latter. How this could be done without increased government intervention he did not say.

Probably Wilson himself was barely conscious of the new path he had found. Certainly his conservative backers were not aware of it. To them he remained the perfect statesman: honest, conservative, and dignified.

George Harvey was probably the first person to spot Wilson's potentialities as a political leader. Harvey, a lean, youthful New Englander, who viewed the world enthusiastically from behind owlish horn-rimmed glasses, had recently become president of the venerable publishing house of Harper and Brothers. He had attended Wilson's inauguration as president of Princeton in 1902 at the invitation of one of the Harpers, principally in order to be present at a dinner party at which Grover Cleveland, Mark Twain, and a number of other luminaries were to appear, but Wilson's speech was the highlight of his visit. It impressed him deeply. The next day he told his secretary: "Get me everything that Woodrow Wilson has written, or that has been written about him," and before he had progressed very far through this literature he had decided that here was the man to revive the fortunes of the Democratic Party, so depressed since the retirement of Cleveland in 1893.

Harvey was a shrewd and knowledgeable politician. Instead of rushing prematurely into a campaign that would have no chance of success, he began to prepare the ground slowly. He published articles in *Harper's Weekly* and in the *North American Review* (which he also controlled) calling for a revival of the Democratic Party under leadership of the Wilson type. He did not mention Wilson, in fact he named no names at all, but he gradually sketched a picture of a presidential candidate—conservative, learned, cultured, perhaps a Southerner of courtly manners, deeply respectful of the traditions of Jefferson, Madison, and Monroe. When, suddenly, at a dinner in Wilson's honor at New York's Lotos Club in 1906, Harvey proposed Wilson as the new leader of the Party, his listeners viewed the suggestion as a happy inspiration. How fortunate that he had thought of Dr. Wilson, who so perfectly fitted the specifications that he (and they) had set up for such a man!

Of course Harvey was merely sending out feelers, but the response was most encouraging. Shortly thereafter he published a picture of Wilson on the cover of *Harper's Weekly*, and reprinted the Lotos Club speech. Newspapers all over the country were soon discussing Wilson as possible presidential timber.

Wilson himself was at once pleased, puzzled, and somewhat disquieted by Harvey's actions. He would certainly like to be president, but the possibility seemed remote at best. Why should Harvey, whom he scarcely knew, bother himself to such a degree about *him*? Besides, talk of Wilson as a politician was bound to produce difficulties at Princeton, where, by this time, he was having difficulties enough. He conferred with Harvey in New York in December 1906, but failed to convince the editor that he should abandon his campaign. So he issued a public statement disclaiming presidential ambitions, and let the matter drop. Harvey continued his work, collected an impressive list of wealthy and influential supporters, and waited.

By the next year Wilson had come around somewhat to Harvey's way of thinking. He met with a group of conservative businessmen and editors and convinced them of the "soundness" of his views. He consented to an abortive scheme to procure the support of New Jersey Democrats for his candidacy for the United States Senate in 1907, which (since the Republicans controlled the legislature) was no more than a cynical attempt to give him a political background and call him to the attention of the voters. He made more and more speeches blasting at Republicans in general and the radicalism of Theodore Roosevelt in particular. As time passed he acted more and more like a candidate and less and less like a college president, though his growing Princeton problems left him little time for politicking.

Harvey, who never doubted that Wilson would decide in favor of politics, matured his plans. By 1909 he was ready. His timetable was simplicity itself. In 1910 Wilson would be elected governor of New Jersey; two years later he would move into the White House.

Until the great depression of the nineties, New Jersey had been a Democratic state, but the political upheavals of that era had tossed it into Republican hands. Big business ruled the day after 1895, and the state became notorious for the laxity of its laws governing corporations. A

Republican reform movement in the early years of the
new century collapsed in 1907, and with the Democrats
boss-ridden and discouraged, the state remained firmly in
conservative control. Harvey had no desire to change this,
but he reasoned that the time was ripe for a swing to the
Democrats. Wilson was the perfect instrument to effect
this change. He could overcome the reputation for "un-
sound," emotional radicalism which the Democratic
Party had developed under the leadership of Bryan, and
at the same time, being a man of unquestioned respecta-
bility, he would escape the charge of being boss- and
machine-dominated.

In January 1910 Harvey met with James Smith, Jr.,
the Democratic boss of New Jersey, whose word could
make or break any gubernatorial candidate. Their conference took place at Delmonico's restaurant in New
York City. Smith was outwardly a far cry from the
coarse, cigar-smoking, derby-hatted, loud-mouthed type
of political leader common in his day. Big, handsome,
immaculately and tastefully dressed, he radiated charm
and distinction. Actually he was a self-made man, the
son of Irish immigrants, who began life as a clerk in his
father's grocery store. But without much formal education
he had risen to great heights. He was the owner of two
newspapers, he was a bank president, and he was the
head of several businesses. Starting his political career as
a Newark alderman, he had prospered phenomenally. In
Cleveland's time he had served a term as United States
senator, and by 1910 he was the recognized ruler of his
party in New Jersey.

It was not easy to convince Smith that Wilson, whom
he called a "Presbyterian priest," would make an acceptable governor. Would he "go along" with the organization? Could he put himself across with "the boys"? But

Harvey was persuasive, and after considering the question for a couple of weeks, Smith agreed. "Well," he
told Harvey finally, "I have thought it all over carefully, and I am ready to go the whole hog." If Wilson
would accept the nomination, Smith would see that it was
offered him.

When confronted with Smith's pledge, Wilson refused to make a definite promise that he would accept
the call. All he would say was that he would give it
"very serious consideration" if it came totally unsolicited,
and without opposition. This sufficed for the time being,
but by June 1910 Smith was demanding a more concrete statement. Some of his henchmen were growing
restive, and other candidates were preparing to enter the
lists. Still Wilson hesitated. By then the Princeton situation had become intolerable, but he felt an obligation to
those trustees who had stood by him through the graduate school fight. These friends, however, quickly gave
him their blessings. Even so, he could not make up his
mind. Why were these politicians so eager to give him
so high an honor? He asked them point blank, but received no satisfactory explanation. Harvey finally called
a group of party leaders to meet with Wilson. One by
one they assured the reluctant candidate that they wanted
him, and that he could win the election.

Wilson eventually decided (naïvely, as he himself
later realized) "that these gentlemen recognized the fact
that a new day had come in American politics, and that
they would have to conduct them[selves] henceforth
after a new fashion." Thus convinced that they had no
ulterior motive, he agreed to run. The announcement
was made on July 15.

Of course, Smith and his associates had come to no
such conclusion. They supported Wilson because they

thought he, and only he, could bring them victory. When someone asked one of the bosses if Wilson would make a good governor, he replied: "How the hell do I know. . . . He will make a good candidate, and that is the only thing that interests me." Smith, like Harvey, was convinced that Wilson could be elected President in 1912; he had visions of playing Mark Hanna to Wilson's McKinley; he saw an avalanche of rich federal patronage descending upon New Jersey. Wilson knew little of the political game, and had assured the bosses he would not attempt to supplant their organization with one of his own. He would be a respectable front, who would, Smith felt sure, leave the "petty details" of political management in the hands of "experienced" men like himself. The boss therefore set the wheels of his machine in motion for the purpose of nominating Wilson.

That Smith was able to marshal enough votes in the state convention in September to nominate Wilson easily was a tribute only to the efficiency of his machine. For almost no one actively desired Wilson's candidacy. The run-of-the-mill party hacks scarcely knew his name and were, in addition, instinctively suspicious of any highbrow amateur. They fell in line only out of loyalty to the organization. As for the liberal minority in the party, they were outspoken in opposition. Led by men like Joseph P. Tumulty of Jersey City and James Kerney, editor of the *Trenton Evening Times*, they fought Wilson with all their strength. They fumed when Wilson refused to commit himself on important questions such as the establishment of an effective public utilities commission, direct primaries, and workmen's compensation laws. They sneered when he issued a statement on organized labor in which he accused the liberals of "wilful and deliberate misrepresentations" of his labor views and then proceeded to reverse these views almost completely in an effort to win labor support. Wilson, Kerney argued, was "a catspaw" serving "the purposes of the bosses." But Smith had the votes.

It was no walkaway. Hot words were exchanged as the liberals raised the charge of "bargain and sale and the double cross," and Wilson's majority on the first ballot was barely one hundred in a total vote of nearly 1,400. But it was victory for the machine nonetheless. "Of all the delegates from Essex County," Smith's lieutenant, James R. Nugent, told Kerney, "there is just one for Wilson; that's the Big Fellow himself." But the huge Essex delegation voted almost to a man as the "Big Fellow" directed.

With the nomination concluded, the convention was about to break up when the dramatic announcement was made that Wilson was en route to the scene to address the delegates. Impatiently the delegates waited. Finally he appeared, pushing his way through the crowd to the rostrum.

The amateur, making his maiden speech as a candidate for office before an audience of unsympathetic, hardened professionals, was a complete success. He wore a dark-gray sack suit with a golf sweater instead of a vest, and his manner of speaking was equally casual. He promised (as all good candidates must) to stand solidly behind the party platform, but he also issued a ringing declaration of independence from boss control. "I shall enter upon the duties of the office of Governor, if elected, with absolutely no pledge of any kind to prevent me from serving the people," he announced. At the finish of his short address the delegates were on their feet, shaking the auditorium with their cheers.

But it was not what Wilson said that stirred his listen-

ers. It was his manner. Here, for the first time, his un-
canny ability to put himself across before large audiences
was given a worthy test. Young Joe Tumulty, bitter, defeated, and discouraged by the machine victory, was in
the crowd. His whole life was changed by that one
speech. "How simple the man, how modest, how cultured!" he later recalled. "Attempting none of the cheap
'plays' of the old campaign orator, he impressively proceeded with his thrilling speech, carrying his audience
under the spell of his eloquent words. How tense the
moment! . . . Only a few sentences are uttered and
our souls are stirred to their very depths."

The bosses made possible Wilson's nomination, but it
was his own ability to convert liberals like Tumulty to
his cause that won him the election. And more than oratory was necessary to gain and keep the liberals. A great
speech might sway them momentarily; over the long pull
from September to election day specific promises were
essential. These, after some hesitation, Wilson provided.
By the time the campaign reached its climax the great
disciple of Edmund Burke was saying: "I am and always have been an insurgent."

The mind of man is a labyrinth through whose complexities the biographer stumbles almost blindly in search
of motives and true emotions. Picture Wilson, plunged
into the excitement of his first campaign. Read his
speeches. Study his itinerary as he tours the state, confers
with local bigwigs, rides through crowds, smiles for the
photographers. Listen, as he says at Asbury Park: "I
want to say, parenthetically, that if you find out that I
have been or ever intend to be connected with a machine
of any kind I hope you will vote against me." But note
that as he speaks Boss Smith and George Harvey are sitting complacently in the audience, and remember that

Jim Nugent is his constant companion as he moves from town to town. Observe him in secret consultation with the bosses while they brief him on the local situation in Mercer County; then watch as he discourses glibly and learnedly with the Mercer ward-heelers about their "problems." See him, "plain, unaffected, affable," as he tells Tumulty how impressed he has been by Tumulty's work for reform in the state legislature, and asks earnestly for suggestions on how better to conduct his campaign.

Or watch him abandon a dozen long-held convictions in the course of a couple of speeches. See him come out for anti-trust legislation, the direct primary, a powerful public service commission, and the direct election of senators. Notice finally, how, under the goad of Republican criticism of his machine connections, he announces: "I shall not, either in the matter of appointments to office or assent to legislation . . . submit to the dictation of any person or persons, special interest or organization. . . . I should deem myself forever disgraced should I in even the slightest degree co-operate [with] . . . the 'boss' system. I regard myself as pledged to the regeneration of the Democratic party."

Is this a mere weathercock of a man, pivoting to accommodate the ever-strengthening progressive breezes of 1910? Is he a subtle hypocrite, mouthing liberal platitudes before the multitude while the Big Fellow and his crew lounge comfortably in the wings? Or has some latent force, long sheltered in his narrow academic background, been suddenly released by the arguments of honest men, or by the cheering throngs so responsive to his eloquence?

Many thoughtful people pondered these questions during the campaign, and it is clear that most of them decided Wilson's change of heart was sincere, for on election day he was swept into office by a large majority. Undoubtedly they judged him rightly; in office he kept his pledges, sloughed off his connections with Smith, and pushed through his newly espoused reforms. He may have begun his startling swing to the left with intentions discreditable to the lofty idealism of his speeches, but before the leaves had fallen from the Princeton elms he had become the prisoner of his own rhetoric, deeply and permanently stirred by the effect that his words had wrought upon the people. Their cheers, reverberating through countless auditoriums, committed his conscience and his fervid Presbyterian soul to causes that his mind had first adopted with, perhaps, unworthy motives.

Poor Boss Smith. When Wilson made his last speech of the campaign, announcing that he would interpret his election as a mandate to assume personal leadership of the party and make war upon the bosses, the Big Fellow wept.

IV

JAMES SMITH, JR., did not hate Woodrow Wilson. Wilson smashed his political career, but Smith could never think of him with any emotion less friendly than mystification. "Wonderful man, wonderful mind, wonderful fighter," he would muse, "but . . ." And the Big Fellow was enough of a realist to shrug his shoulders and give up the painful struggle to understand.

Smith's trouble was that he was a politician. Like most politicians he had a "professional" attitude toward others of his kind and toward the public. He was bound to most of the members of his guild (Republican as well as Democrat) by mutually held loyalties and sympathies, and by a common awareness of the peculiar problems involved in winning and holding office, organizing legislative programs, and dealing with that fickle, pliable, powerful, and somewhat mysterious force, "the public." Long experience had led him to believe that practical results depended upon getting along with one's colleagues, and that to do this one must make concessions to their foibles, prejudices, and particular needs. Sometimes one must say things to "the public" that were, if not exactly false, at least misleading. Of course the politician must *talk* principles and public duty when addressing the public. The public (strange entity) expected its politicians to act like "statesmen." But with his fellows (realists like himself) the politician need not dissemble.

Wilson simply did not fit this pattern. He played the politician to perfection in his public relations. Smith had watched him campaign with frank admiration, the perfect "statesman." But Wilson insisted on acting like a statesman with the politicians as well. Not knowing that this was against the rules, that it would not work, he blithely proceeded to make it work, at least for a time. Some of the politicians were deeply offended. They called Wilson an ingrate and a hypocrite. Smith, being of a philosophical turn of mind, did not react emotionally. But he was sorely puzzled.

The Big Fellow was intelligent enough to realize, even while the campaign was still in progress, that Wilson meant what he said about fighting the machine. But habit, if nothing else, made him act in the interval between November and the beginning of Wilson's term in mid-January as though a "normal" governor had been chosen. Contrary to all expectations, Wilson's popularity with the voters had pulled a majority of Democratic candidates for the state legislature into office. Thus, for the first time in nearly twenty years, the Democrats would be able to name a United States senator. Smith himself had been the last one, and he had left office under a cloud. It seems that he had purchased a thousand shares of a sugar stock when a tariff bill was under discussion, and had then played a leading part in a fight to raise the tariff on sugar. Now he was getting on in years, and he wished to clear his name and round out his career by serving another term in the Senate.

During the gubernatorial campaign, when Wilson's foes had been stressing his machine connections, Smith had offered to withdraw from the Senate race, but Wilson, who hated to deal with any issue in terms of personalities, had not pressed him to do so. The question at the time seemed academic, since no one expected the Democrats to carry the legislature. But after election day, when Smith informed Wilson that he intended to go ahead, the Governor-elect objected strongly. If he ran, Wilson pointed out, "all the ugliest suspicions of the campaign" would be revived. Further, there had been a Senate preferential primary during the summer. Smith had not bothered to enter it, and it had been won by James E. Martine, the "Farmer Orator" of Plainfield.

Wilson admitted that the primary had been a farce. Only a small fraction of the voters had participated in it. He also admitted that Martine, a well-meaning, but loquacious and rather muddleheaded follower of Bryan, was unfit for the office. ("The trouble with Martine as a talker is that he has no terminal facilities," Wilson once confessed.) He therefore suggested to Smith that a "compromise" candidate be found, acceptable to all members of the party.

This was a serious error, for he was soon barraged by his liberal supporters with demands that he fight for the principle of direct election of senators, which he had supported in the campaign. Impressed by their logic, he gave up all thought of abandoning Martine. He tried to work on Smith through their mutual friend, Harvey. Smith, Wilson told the editor, would make a fine senator, but the voters were convinced that he was dishonest. "It is grossly unjust that they should regard Senator Smith as the impersonation of all that they hate and fear; but they do, and there's an end to the matter." Thus, though he would "sincerely deplore" it, as a matter of duty he would have to fight Smith if he persisted in running. "I have had to do similar things in the University," he added meaningfully. "By the same token—ridiculous though it undoubtedly is—I think we shall have to stand by Mr. Martine."

Smith and Harvey discussed the problem in detail. It was clear that in a fight to the finish on this question, Wilson would be the winner. But in his own way, the

Big Fellow was also a man of principle. "Well, by God," he finally told Harvey, "I guess I'll let him beat me." And beat him Wilson did—overwhelmingly. He conferred individually with almost every Democrat in the legislature; he issued a public statement denouncing Smith and supporting Martine; he summoned Smith's closest friends to Princeton and lectured them on their obligations to the public. Without resorting to conventional political pressures, without threats or promises of jobs, he persuaded even some of the Essex legislators to desert their leader. His very unconventionality was his strongest weapon. "He is a great man," one somewhat stunned assemblyman muttered after an interview with Wilson. "He talked to us as a father would."

The showdown came in the new legislature on January 25, 1911. Martine won easily; Smith received only three votes. "I pitied Smith at the last," Wilson commented later. "It was so plain that he had so few real friends. . . . The minute it was seen that he was defeated his adherents began to desert him like rats leaving a sinking ship."

The victory over Smith assured the new Governor of control of his own party, and thus made possible the enactment of a program of liberal reform. Had Smith retained his influence in the legislature this could not have been. Yet it was Wilson's *management* of his new power that converted the mere possibility into accomplished fact.

Wilson continually amazed the professionals by his lack of interest in patronage, supposedly the very lifeblood of politics. He made one basic decision at the start of his administration—that patronage would be controlled by the progressive wing of the party—and put the entire matter into the hands of James Kerney and Jo-

seph Tumulty, whom he had appointed as his private
secretary. Then he dismissed the subject from his mind
so completely that he seldom knew even the names of
persons filling minor political positions in the state.
"What have we been doing for Blank that he has been
in here thanking me so profusely?" he asked Kerney one
day. Kerney explained, to Wilson's vast amusement,
that "Blank" was holding down a comfortable job under
a gubernatorial appointment in the state house itself.

But if Wilson tended to ignore the politicians, his
handling of the public was masterly. The door of his office was always open, and, in the Jeffersonian tradition,
he tried to make himself accessible to all citizens. Oswald
Garrison Villard of the *Nation* was deeply impressed
when he visited Trenton and found the Governor wandering about in his outer office chatting informally with
visitors. "There are no fuss and feathers where he is,"
Villard recorded. Wilson also made a great effort in his
public speeches to get across to the people the broad implications of the many issues he discussed. "Do you recognize the significance of this meeting?" he asked one
audience during a discussion of municipal reform. "We
are here to discuss a matter of principle that concerns the
city of Trenton, but we are really here discussing a trans-
action that concerns mankind." Or, on another occasion:
"Do not leave this hall thinking the issues of Atlantic
county are merely the issues of Atlantic county. Do not
forget that you are Americans. Do not forget that the
American character is in your keeping."

Wilson did this sort of thing superbly, but he did it at
great cost to himself. He was not by nature a "hand-
shaker," or a "baby-kisser." And he was intolerant of
stupidity and dullness, a great deal of which he had to
tolerate every day of his term. His home life, always his

bulwark and his citadel, almost disappeared. "I have no private life at all," he complained to a friend. "It is entertaining to see the whole world surge about you . . . but when a fellow is like me—when, i.e., he loves his own privacy, loves the liberty to think of his friends (live with them in his thought, if he can have them no other way) and to dream his own dreams— . . . rebellion comes into his heart and he flings about like a wild bird in a cage." The constant attendance of aides and flunkies, the brass bands, the gaping sightseers, and the parades of visiting dignitaries were almost more than he could bear. For Ellen Wilson, whose life was in the home, and who had found even her duties as first lady of Princeton a strain on her shy, retiring nature, the pressure was even worse, and this added to the burden of her doting husband. "Where and when does one's heart get a chance to breathe and to call up the sweet memories and dreams upon which it lives?" he lamented.

Yet from the broils and tumult of which he complained he drew the strength to save himself. The very crowds that destroyed his privacy brought him, through their cheers, to a new awareness of his public obligations. "All sorts and conditions of people came," he wrote, describing the big receptions that followed his inauguration. "I felt very close to all of them, and very much touched by the thought that I was their representative and spokesman, and in a very real sense their help and hope. . . . I have felt a sort of solemnity in it all that I feel sure will not wear off. I do not see how a man in such a position could possibly be afraid of anything except failing to do his honourable duty." The feeling did not wear off, and there was never danger that Woodrow Wilson would be derelict in the performance of his "honourable duty."

Wilson's brilliant handling of the public, however, is not enough to explain his success as governor. Laws are made by legislators, and while public opinion can sometimes be held over their reluctant heads, an executive who wishes to push through a large and complicated program requires something more. Of course, despite his personal lack of interest in patronage, the bait of gubernatorial appointments was held out effectively to legislators by Kerney and Tumulty. Wilson himself concentrated on less usual techniques.

Realizing that he could not count upon the Smith machine, he turned to progressives of both parties for help. This brought anguished cries from many Democratic "regulars" but added to his prestige with the people of the state. He also set up a steering committee to outline a legislative timetable, and then, like the prime minister he wished to be, he took up his plans before the Democratic legislators, meeting in caucus, arguing, cajoling, striving in every way to maintain party unanimity. When Jim Nugent, circulating through committee rooms and collaring representatives on the floor of the assembly, tried to sabotage the program, Wilson first warned him politely to stop, and then, when Nugent persisted, he summoned him to his office and ordered him to desist. Nugent flatly refused, and, with Wilson's temper rising, accused him of misusing patronage to force his will upon the legislature. "Good afternoon, Mr. Nugent," Wilson said with cold fury, ushering him from his office with a wave of his hand. A contemporary cartoon showing Nugent catapulting head first from the office, propelled by a foot marked "Wilson," portrayed vividly the spirit of the interview, if not the actual fact.

This kind of leadership was effective in the lower house of the legislature; in the Senate, where the Repub-

licans had retained a thin majority of the seats, more subtle techniques were required. Acting on Tumulty's advice, Wilson invited both Democratic and Republican
Senate leaders to a stag dinner at the Trenton Country
Club. Tumulty had urged the Governor to try to overcome his natural stiffness and reserve with strangers, and
for once Wilson was able to do so. A delicious fried-
chicken-and-waffle dinner may have helped, but in any
case he was less restrained than he had ever been outside
his family.

The party was a spectacular success. One Republican
senator made a comical speech, much interrupted by
jibes and wisecracks, in which he said to Wilson that
"the trouble" was not that he loved Wilson more, but
that Wilson loved him less. Wilson retorted: "Whom
the Lord loveth he chasteneth," and then, in Wilson's
words, "we were off!" There was a three-piece band for
music, and soon the whole party was prancing about in
high glee. Wilson and one of the Republican leaders led
the company in a cakewalk, and, as Wilson said afterwards: "The rest of the evening was one unbroken
romp."

"The senators are as jolly as boys when they let themselves 'go,'" he noted. The same was true of himself.
While no one can assess the effect of this dinner directly, it must have helped Wilson in his relations with
the upper house. In any case, within the short span of
six weeks the legislature had approved Wilson's entire
program, and more besides. On March 13 he met with
the Democratic caucus to open his offensive. On April
23 the legislature adjourned, its work completed.

The changes wrought were impressive. Perhaps most
important was the revision of the procedure governing
elections, aimed at destroying the boss system. Direct

primaries replaced the convention system of nomination for all elected officials, election boards were placed under civil service, and voters in the cities were required to register personally. State publication of official ballots replaced the old method, which left this important task to the parties. Candidates were forced to submit detailed statements of their expenses, which were limited by law, and corporations were prohibited from contributing to any candidate's campaign fund. The extent to which corruption had eaten into the old system was brought out by a law providing for the mailing of sample ballots to all registered voters. When this was first done in Newark in 1911, eleven thousand were returned by the post office as undeliverable. They had been addressed to vacant lots, persons long dead, and the like.

Another new law established an effective public utilities commission, which was empowered to fix rates, set standards, and control the finances of all common carriers and of light, heat, power, water, and telephone companies. In addition, an employers' liability act was passed that protected workers in case of on-the-job injury. The legislature went even beyond Wilson's comprehensive program, passing laws that regulated the labor of women and children, controlled the storage and processing of food, and improved the school system.

"I got absolutely everything I strove for—and more besides," Wilson confided happily to a friend. "The result was as complete a victory as has ever been won, I venture to say, in the history of the country. . . . I kept the pressure of opinion constantly on the legislature, and the programme was carried out to its last detail." As Wilson himself admitted, New Jersey had been long ready for such reforms. "I came to the office in the fulness of time, when opinion was ripe on all these matters," he said. But it was his leadership which was decisive. "It's a great game, thoroughly worth playing!" His ex-ultation was understandable.

But his moment of triumph was brief. Wilson's star had risen so rapidly and so high in New Jersey by the spring of 1911 that a reaction was inevitable. The kind of pressure he exerted on the politicos could not be main-tained indefinitely; the enthusiasm he inspired among the voters was bound to wane, especially as their sense of outrage at the bosses and the "interests" dissolved into complacency as a result of Wilson's achievements. Old loyalties and old habits gradually revived. Boss Smith and his colleagues, swept aside by Wilson's first grand charge, were now to turn the remnants of their battered forces to the work of sabotage. And Wilson, tempera-mentally unsuited for waging a defensive war, played a part in his own downfall.

In November 1911 the Republicans regained control of the legislature, chiefly because of Democratic defec-tions in Essex County, where Smith and Nugent ob-tained their revenge. Wilson was unable to work harmo-niously with a dominant opposition party. In the 1912 session he vetoed nearly all the important legislation sent to his desk, hurling epithets like "scandalous," "arbi-trary," and "dangerous" at the Republican majorities. "Wilson," comments Professor Arthur S. Link, "re-vealed his temperamental inability to cooperate with men who were not willing to follow his lead completely; he had not lost his habit, long since demonstrated at Prince-ton, of making his political opponents also his personal enemies, whom he despised and loathed. He had to hold the reins and do the driving alone; it was the only kind of leadership he knew."

But, as was the case when trouble had developed at

Princeton, failure led only to greater success. On that occasion Wilson had abandoned an untenable position and
drawn up his lines anew at Trenton. Now, outflanked
again, he boldly crossed the Delaware and marched on to
Washington and the White House.

The *Wilson for President* movement, originating in
the imagination of George Harvey, had developed a
good deal of conservative backing before 1911. But
Wilson's swing to progressivism and his attack on Boss
Smith cost him most of this support. However, as fast as
the "original Wilson men" withdrew, new "original
Wilson men" filled their places, for it was apparent now
that he was first-class presidential timber.

The new Wilsonians were not conservatives, but they
were no more radical than their candidate. Like him,
most were middle-of-the-roaders: editors, businessmen,
lawyers; many of them were Southerners, drawn to Wilson by his honesty, level-headed idealism, and respecta-
bility. They saw him as a Bryan, with dignity and brains
added, and minus Bryan's radicalism and eccentricity.

The most important of these backers were Walter
Hines Page, William F. McCombs, and William G.
McAdoo. (Colonel House, though an early ally, did
not play much of a part until the campaign was over.)
All three men were from the South. Page, after a classical education that included two years at Johns Hopkins,
had done distinguished work as a newspaperman, as editor of the *Forum*, the *Atlantic Monthly*, and *World's
Work*, and as a partner in the publishing house of Dou-
bleday, Page and Company. He was well known for his
campaign to revitalize the South through educational im-
provements, scientific agriculture, and the promotion of
industry. Though always a Democrat, he had never sup-

ported Bryan. McCombs was from Arkansas. A student
of Wilson's at Princeton, he had gone on to the Harvard
Law School and set up practice in New York. Unlike
Page, who was of a whimsical nature, McCombs was intense, introverted, and ambitious. Crippled in body from
early life, with a mind that was also somehow warped,
given increasingly during the campaign to fits of jeal-
ousy and to physical collapse, he nonetheless was a key
figure, for he understood politics and politicians as did
none of his colleagues. It was his work in raising money
and building up local organizations that provided the
framework for victory. McAdoo, a relatively late addition to the group, had made a name for himself in the
construction of the first tunnel under the Hudson River.
He was a lean, rather ugly Georgian, with a long neck
and a nose like a bird of prey. His energy, common sense,
and superb ability as an organizer, together with his financial connections, made him increasingly important in the
course of the campaign.

Wilson's managers worked devotedly, but they encountered all sorts of disheartening obstacles, for being a
moderate, Wilson was sniped at from all sides. Dozens
of hostile eyes scanned his past record eagerly. And of
course it was vulnerable. Someone uncovered a letter,
written in 1907, in which he had expressed the desire
"to knock Mr. Bryan once and for all into a cocked hat."
Since Bryan could generally make or break any Democratic hopeful, this disclosure could have been cata-
strophic. ("If I wrote what I think of that man," Wilson
said later, referring to the suspected source of the letter's
publication, "it would have to be on asbestos.") Fortunately Bryan's magnanimity was as unbounded as his self-
regard. He refused to take offense, and Wilson repaired
the damage in a striking speech in praise of "the charac-

ter and the devotion and the preaching of William Jennings Bryan."

No sooner had this crisis subsided than George Harvey precipitated another. Irked by Wilson's frank affirmative answer when asked if the support of *Harper's Weekly* was injuring his chances, Harvey dramatically struck Wilson's name from the masthead of his magazine. There was much unjust talk of Wilson's "ingratitude," but when the full story was known (Harvey had, after all, asked Wilson for his honest opinion), this affair also worked to the candidate's advantage.

There were other difficulties. It came out late in 1911 that Wilson had applied to the Carnegie Foundation for an annuity after his resignation from Princeton. Critics pointed out that such pensions were for indigent *teachers,* not indigent politicians, and from the left came thundering denunciations of anyone who would seek the largesse of the great steel baron. Then the Hearst press began combing Wilson's *History of the American People,* written while he was still a conservative, for opinions that would injure his chances. Damaging, and what was worse, accurate quotations were splashed across the pages of Hearst's many papers, illustrating Wilson's contempt for strikers, radical farm organizations, recent Italian and Hungarian immigrants, and advocates of cheap money. To Hearst's attacks were added frenzied outpourings of filth and lies from the pen of Thomas E. Watson of Georgia. Watson, whose paper spoke for the ignorant, Negro-hating "cracker" element, even claimed to see danger of the domination of America by the Pope in the fact that Joseph Tumulty, Wilson's secretary, was a Catholic.

Wilson fought off these attacks, fair and foul alike, as best he could. Indeed, on occasion, he twisted, ducked, dodged, and squirmed like the most agile of the profes-

sional politicians. He mouthed platitudes about democracy while he equivocated on controversial issues. (He
told his "fellow Virginians," for example, that *they* did
not need the initiative, referendum, and recall, because
these reforms were required only where "genuine representative government" did not exist. Yet "genuine repre
sentative government" was as much a stranger to Virginia in 1911 as it is today.) He apologized profusely
to immigrant groups aroused by passages in his *History*,
and promised to remove the offensive words in the next
edition. Gradually but inevitably he learned the bitter
truth—that no one gets to the White House without pay-
ing a price in surrendered principles.

Of course the seamy side of Wilson's campaign should
not be exaggerated. If he was often vague and contradictory on specific issues, his new faith in the people was
unfeigned. His campaign was dignified and earnest. Being inexperienced, he was not always efficient. Sometimes he was downright confused. But he conveyed his
basic message to the voters. His fortunes rose, fell, and
rose again, but when the Democratic delegates gathered
in Baltimore in June 1912 for the nominating convention, Wilson had a solid core of some 250 votes with
hopes of picking up many others. He was not the leader,
but he was in a strong position.

The 1912 Democratic convention was long-drawn-
out and tense. It developed into a fight between Wilson
and Champ Clark of Missouri, with Clark leading from
the start but never able to obtain the two-thirds majority
then required for nomination. Clark was Speaker of the
House of Representatives. Throughout a long career, he
had been a consistent liberal, a loyal follower of Bryan.
But he was also accustomed to the give and take of professional politics. He was on good terms with the boss-

dominated machine organizations, whereas Bryan would
not stomach them. Like Bryan, he was the spellbinder
type of orator, and rather eccentric (he once gave a testi-
monial for a concoction named Electric Bitters: "The
best all-round medicine ever sold over a druggist's
counter"); unlike Bryan, he was a heavy and habitual
drinker. Although he had been president of a college before entering politics, he was essentially an unintellectual,
rural politician. Wilson called him, with much justice,
"a sort of elephantine 'smart Aleck.' "

Clark's drive had been checked by the eleventh ballot. When, a little later, Bryan broke with him because
Tammany Hall had thrown New York's ninety votes
into his column, his fate was sealed. But his strength declined very slowly. There was a protracted deadlock, the
minor candidates holding out in hopes that the lightning
would strike one of them. Wilson waited, seemingly un-
concerned, at the governor's summer mansion at Sea
Girt. Resolutely he refused his managers' pleas that he
make promises of future favors in return for votes. In the
end the managers made the necessary commitments without his knowledge. Boss-dominated votes in Illinois and
Indiana swung the balance finally, and then the minor
candidates pushed him over the top. On the forty-sixth
ballot the convention nominated Woodrow Wilson for
President of the United States.

Wilson accepted the result calmly. When William F.
McCombs and the Democratic National Committee
came to Sea Girt to congratulate him, he shook their
hands gravely and said: "McCombs, you know I am a
Presbyterian and believe in predestination. . . . It was
Providence that did the work at Baltimore." Providence
—on the forty-sixth ballot. McCombs felt a chill run up
his spine. "I stood there a complete wreck from a cam-

paign at Baltimore, during which I slept no more than two hours a night," he recorded later. "I saw other drawn faces about me. . . . I could not accept Wilson's view of fore-ordination."

Fate had little to do with Wilson's nomination, but once nominated, he was predestined to be elected. For the social ferment that had convulsed America since the turn of the century, that Bryan had first unleashed and Theodore Roosevelt made respectable, that had transformed Wilson into a militant liberal almost overnight, had reached its peak. The progressive movement, born in the depression of the nineties, and fed by the complex problems resulting from industrialization, by 1912 had split the Republican party in two. The Old Guard retained control and renominated President Taft. The liberals then broke away, set up the Progressive party, and named Roosevelt as their candidate. For the Democrats, united behind the popular Wilson, victory was almost certain.

Thus, although the three-cornered campaign was hotly contested, it was important only in its effect on Wilson. He was now a truly national figure. When the news of his nomination reached Sea Girt he sent a man out to buy a box of cigars. "That's the first box of cigars Woodrow ever bought," remarked Ellen Wilson. Ellen was a shrewd politician and recognized the significance of the event.

There followed, as Wilson himself put it, "an invasion by the people of the United States." For a time it was nearly more than he could endure—reporters, delegations, speeches without end. "The life I am leading now can't keep up," he wrote in mid-July. "Not a moment am I left free to do what I would. I thought last night that I should go crazy with the strain and confusion

of it." The newspapermen in particular irritated him.
Their wisecracking cynicism and brash, even vulgar, manners he found abhorrent. He was offended when they
asked him for an advance copy of a speech because the
wires would be jammed later with reports of a World
Series game. When he tried to joke with them, they distorted his words to make flashy headlines. Once, in explaining how he was falling behind in answering his
mail, he said that he felt like the frog in the well. "Every
time he jumped up one foot he fell back two." The next
day a New York paper displayed this headline: WILSON
FEELS LIKE A FROG. Another time a bold correspondent told him: "We are all on space down here, Governor, and the more we can play you up the more we
can increase our checks at the end of the week." His hor-
ror at the casual cynicism of the journalists did not escape
these practiced observers. William Allen White remem-
bered Wilson's first handshake. It felt "like a ten-cent
pickled mackerel in brown paper," completely lacking
in human warmth. "He had a highty-tighty way that re-
pulsed me," White said. "When he tried to be pleasant
he creaked."

Wilson never learned how to handle the press, but
the excitement, the cheers, and the challenge of the occasion toughened him amazingly. He found that he could
get along with at least some of the machine politicians
who, scenting victory, suddenly found him very attrac-
tive, although he leaned heavily on Tumulty in dealing
with them. He even consented to record a few "canned"
speeches, which for some reason he considered undignified. As the campaign approached its climax, he wrote:
"It is wonderful how tough I have turned out to be, and
how much I can stand." Indeed, despite the physical and
mental strain, he actually put on weight between June

and November, and emerged from the test more fit than he had been in years.

On election day Wilson was at Princeton. His wife and daughters and a few intimates were with him. He voted in the morning, and took a long walk after lunch with a few of his friends. They wandered through the countryside, and strolled about the campus. He showed them the diploma of James Madison, still for the moment the only Princeton graduate to reach the White House. After a quiet dinner, the little group gathered to wait. Ellen Wilson read aloud the poems of Robert Browning. At ten a telegraph operator handed her a bit of paper. Woodrow Wilson had been elected President of the United States.

Near by, the president of Princeton University, Wilson's lost friend, Jack Hibben, sat through the vigil at Prospect. When the news reached him, he gave an order. A few minutes later the ancient bell of Nassau Hall tolled its bitter-sweet message across the darkened campus.

V

A MAN of Wilson's intense nature, so dependent upon nervous energy, was bound to suffer a reaction when the excitement of the campaign was over. The mere prospect of being President of the United States, with all the public problems and personal adjustments it would entail, was enough to shake him. "The time has come to do a lot of thinking," he announced the day after election.

But in New Jersey thought was impossible. Fifteen thousand letters descended upon Princeton in a few days. Like hungry jackals, the politicians gathered. The day after election McCombs was on hand with a complete Cabinet in his pocket. The only salvation lay in flight. Taking his immediate family and a single stenographer, Wilson went to Bermuda for a month of rest and preparation, announcing that no decisions would be made until his return.

The weeks there were busy ones, but not hectic, disorganized, and frustrating, as they would have been at home. Wilson took care of his more important letters, worked on preliminary plans for his Cabinet, and gave a great deal of thought to the specific program he would present to Congress in order to implement the generalities of his campaign speeches. On December 16 he was back home, much refreshed. He plunged at once into the complexities of organizing his administration.

In this work he had plenty of help—far more than he desired or could use. He always made his own decisions in the end, but more and more he came to depend upon one man, Colonel Edward M. House.

At Princeton and again at Trenton Wilson displayed

a peculiar ineptness in handling advisers, both friendly and critical. It was not that he would not listen to suggestions. Quite the contrary, his mind soaked up information and ideas no matter what the source. Observers who thought him insensitive to the opinions of others misunderstood him. "I never met a more open-minded man," wrote Joe Tumulty, who dealt with him intimately for eleven years. "I always felt free in every public matter . . . frankly to express my own opinion and openly to disagree with him."

But Wilson placed a tremendous strain on those who tried to help him. *He* must be the leader, *his* the ultimate decision. Moreover, he expected advisers to sacrifice their own opinions once he had determined his own. Members of his Cabinet learned this quickly, and some, like Bryan, resented it. Tumulty did not mind, because he subordinated himself so completely to his chief. "The Governor," as he always thought of his boss, was a sort of a demigod to Tumulty, who never ceased to marvel that he, the son of a humble Irish immigrant, had come to know the great Wilson. While it is true that he often disagreed with Wilson and sometimes persuaded him to change his mind, he was also able to purge his own mind of "heretical" views on the many occasions when Wilson did not accept his advice.

Less self-sacrificing associates, no matter how loyal, often had difficulty in working with Wilson. A number of his Princeton colleagues, like most professors inclined to criticize others and to defend their own opinions, have left records of his egocentric leadership:

"You could work *for*, but not always *with* Wilson."

"He did not explicitly demand but implicitly assumed absolute and exclusive loyalty, and always tested devotion to his cause in terms of personal loyalty to himself."

"It is perhaps as a judge of men that Mr. Wilson shone least in his day-to-day conduct of affairs, being prone to evaluate them for their attitude toward himself, rather than their ability or their competence for the assigned task."

Wilson yearned for friendship, yet seldom dared to give or accept it. "If I make an intimate of a man in politics, it isn't long before he wants me to do something which I ought not to do," he once remarked. Though he could never abandon his own principles for friendship's sake, he commonly expected others to do so.

Colonel House was able to enter into the unique relationship that has been called "The Strangest Friendship in History" because he so thoroughly understood this side of Wilson's nature. House was a Texan, son of a wealthy Houston banker. Politics was his passion; refusal to seek or accept political office the secret of his influence. He was a small, delicate man with a thin, grave face. His eyes, calm yet alert, were like a wild bird's. When he discussed a difficult question he used his hands expressively, "as though he were picking things apart, or pulling them out to look at." Holding some imaginary object in his slender fingers, he would caress the air with delicate soothing motions, as (oh, so reasonably) he described, explained, and interpreted.

House aspired to be a president-maker. By late 1911 he had decided that Wilson was the proper clay with which to realize this ambition. George Harvey provided the necessary introductions, and the two men hit it off from the start. Wilson found in the Texan a man of intelligence, shrewdness, and discretion who was experienced in politics and yet high-minded, urbane yet zealous. But above all he was struck by House's lack of concern for personal gain. "He wants nothing for himself,

He will not hold office and is a truly disinterested friend
—*the most valuable possession a man could have.*"

As a matter of fact Wilson never understood the Colonel. "Mr. House is my second personality," he once said.
"He is my independent self. His thoughts and mine are
one." Wilson meant this literally, but of course he was
wrong in his judgment. It is true that House sought no
more reward than the right to help and influence, but he
neither identified himself with Wilson nor viewed their
relationship uncritically. "I had a delightful visit from
Woodrow Wilson yesterday afternoon," House reported
to his brother-in-law after his first meeting with the Governor in November 1911. "He is not the biggest man I
have ever met, but he is one of the pleasantest, and I
would rather play with him than any prospective candidate I have seen."

House did understand Wilson; at least he understood
him as well as any one man can another. He quickly
sensed Wilson's need for unquestioning loyalty. Being a
thoughtful, objective, and, in his way, ambitious man, he
could not give such loyalty. But he knew when to be silent. "I . . . did not care to discuss an issue after the
decision was made, even if I disagreed with the decision,"
he explained to George Sylvester Viereck. "I never
wasted tears crying over spilt milk." In their discussions,
when Wilson was silent it meant agreement; when
House was silent it meant disagreement. Wilson never
realized this. House always realized it. In one of their in-
numerable conversations Wilson told House that he was
always eager for advice. "I almost laughed at this statement," House recorded in his diary. But he did not actually laugh.

After the election Wilson offered House a post in his
Cabinet. When the offer was refused, House's place in

Wilson's heart was assured. It is significant that House later remarked: "Had I gone into the Cabinet I could not have lasted eight weeks." It is even more significant that he did not say this to Woodrow Wilson.

In the Cabinet that Wilson finally selected, Bryan was Secretary of State, McAdoo Secretary of the Treasury, Lindley M. Garrison head of the War Department, and Josephus Daniels in charge of the Navy Department. James C. McReynolds was Attorney General, Albert S. Burleson Postmaster General, William C. Redfield Secretary of Commerce, Franklin K. Lane head of Interior, and David F. Houston Secretary of Agriculture. William B. Wilson was Secretary of the newly established Labor Department.

Bryan's appointment was a political necessity. Although he made no effort to push his own candidacy, his friends raised a din in his behalf that could not be ignored. Wilson felt that Bryan would be useless in the Cabinet, but although he made a halfhearted effort to persuade him to take a diplomatic post, he accepted the inevitable with good grace. The support of Bryan and especially of his friends in Congress was essential for the success of Wilson's legislative program. McAdoo's selection was a reward for services rendered during the campaign, as was that of Daniels. Burleson, with sixteen years in Congress behind him, was Wilson's choice for the "one thorough-going politician" he felt he must have in his official family. The others were appointed for a variety of reasons; Garrison, for example, was chosen because Tumulty felt that there ought to be a Jerseyite in the Cabinet.

House had a great deal to do with these appointments. He did not actually select the men, but he collected information about dozens of possibilities, digested it, and funneled it on to Wilson. He also negotiated with the politicians, whom Wilson did not want to take into his confidence, and on a number of occasions sounded out individuals whom Wilson was considering seriously. By the time the slate was complete on the eve of the inauguration in March 1913, Wilson's confidence in House was unbounded and the mold of their relationship during the next eight years had been formed. All in all, it was a valuable relationship for Wilson. If House was not always frank, he was still sincerely devoted to his chief, and a constant moderating influence on Wilson's passionate and sometimes impractical nature.

Wilson faced his inauguration on March 4 deeply impressed with his new responsibilities. When an old friend offered congratulations, he asked instead for prayer. "This is not a day of triumph," he said in concluding his brief inaugural speech, "it is a day of dedication." He decided against an inaugural ball, bringing down upon his head the wrath of Washington's shopkeepers and society leaders, and he refused an honorary membership in the Chevy Chase Country Club. All in all, the inauguration was a somber rather than an inspiring event.

But it was an event of enormous significance. It marked a swing of the center of power from the Northeast to the South and West, a complete overturn in the leadership of Congress, and the culmination of twenty years of progressive struggle for reform. And it brought to power a man sometimes less liberal than his public statements indicated, but possessed of tremendous personal force and dedicated to the protection and advancement of the interests of the people.

In Washington, the pattern Wilson had established at Princeton and Trenton was repeated on a larger scale. Once again he accomplished prodigious results in an incredibly short time. Once again his chief advantage was that in times of change and uncertainty he saw clearly what was needed, and knew exactly how he proposed to achieve his goals. Using methods inspiring in their very novelty, he reaffirmed the faith of his followers, capti-vated the doubtful, and overawed the opposition. Within a few days he had stirred public interest by appearing before Congress in person to present his program, some-thing that had not been done since the time of John Adams. In a matter of weeks he had the White House executive offices operating smoothly. In a year he pushed more important legislation through Congress than most of his predecessors had in four.

The move to the larger sphere of Washington did in-volve some changes in method. Wilson could not, for in-stance, maintain his "open-door policy" of admitting ev-eryone to his office. Because of his innate dislike of person-to-person contacts this change was a definite re-lief to him. He soon laid down a rule that he would see no one below Cabinet rank without an appointment, and he encouraged congressmen and government officials to deal with him through letters and memoranda. In a sense this was strange. He avoided communicating with Con-gress in writing because he felt that a speech "carried in-finitely more weight" than a written message, and en-abled the orator to "really get at" his audience. But he did not enjoy being "got at" himself in this way.

"Interviews and consultations," he told a newspaper-man, "lead to nothing except the gratification . . . of those who see me that they have had their say." Once Wilson gave a visiting banker twenty minutes to explain a proposition. For eighteen minutes the banker rambled about on the fringes of his subject while the President squirmed impatiently. Finally Wilson interrupted him,

stating what he took to be the man's argument in a few
succinct phrases. "Is that what you are trying to propose?" he asked. The banker admitted that it was. "I see
nothing in it," Wilson snapped, ending the interview.
He did not realize that ordinary men might lack his own
flashing insights and lightning comprehension, or that
even intelligent and experienced men might be somewhat
overawed in the stately White House executive cham-
bers.

If a visitor could state his case quickly and clearly, he
did not find Wilson cold or indifferent. "Two or three
times," Ray Stannard Baker recalled in his autobiogra-
phy, "when I told him some fact that interested him a
look as of keen appetite came into his face. He pounces
upon things half said and consumes them before they are
well out of one's mind." But such men were rare. For
the majority, those who had "nothing to give" him, Wilson showed only impatience and contempt, and this
made him many enemies. Their ill-feeling was unfair, for
the burdens of office upon his frail physique made wasted
effort intolerable, but it is also true that faith in his mission fostered a sort of remoteness in him. More and more
he enjoyed making the great decisions by himself—alone
with his conscience and his God.

More significant than his growing remoteness was the
President's changed attitude toward party politics. His
experiences in New Jersey undoubtedly paved the way
for this change, but the decisive factor was Wilson's
"thorough-going politician," Postmaster General Burleson.

Soon after he took office Wilson discussed the problem of patronage with Burleson. "Now Burleson," he
announced, "I am going to appoint forward-looking
men and I am going to satisfy myself that they are hon-

est and capable." Burleson shuddered. He saw the administration falling in ruins. He pictured Wilson check-
ing on the 56,000 postmasterships and thousands of
other minor appointments that had to be handed out,
while senators fumed and legislation languished. He
knew also the difficulties involved in arguing with his
chief's tender conscience. "I had to do some fast thinking," he recalled years later. Fortunately, he decided to
take a stand.

"Mr. President," he said firmly, "if you pursue this
policy, it means that your administration is going to be a
failure. . . . It doesn't amount to a damn who is postmaster in Paducah, Kentucky. But these little offices
mean a great deal to the senators and representatives in
Congress." He talked for two hours, and Wilson heard
him out in hostile silence. Finally, the President agreed
to think it over.

A week later he called Burleson back. Again the Postmaster General argued, explained, almost begged him
to understand. At last Wilson gave in. Eventually he
could even joke about minor patronage. Burleson would
come in with a batch of appointments and Wilson, without glancing at them, would smile and say plaintively:
"Where do I sign?"

Of course the significance of his capitulation tran-
scended petty questions of federal patronage. Wilson's
decision to go along with the status quo meant that in
many states he was working with conservative elements
to the detriment of his own liberal friends. But he reaped
the advantages of party loyalty. The party hacks in Congress, their piddling demands satisfied, went along duti-
fully with "orders" from the White House on the big
issues. "My head is with the progressives in the Democratic party, but my heart, because of the way they stood

by me, is with the so-called Old Guard," he told Tumulty. "They stand without hitching." How Boss Smith must have wished that Wilson had adopted this view earlier!

But fundamentally Wilson's executive method was the same as it had been in New Jersey. He saw himself as the voice of the American people and as the leader of Congress in carrying out the people's will. "No one but the President seems to be expected . . . to look out for the general interest of the country," he remarked during his first summer in office. He found no contradiction between this nonpartisan responsibility and his newfound faith in the virtues of co-operating with the Democratic machine politicians. His basic strategy, an outgrowth of his long-held belief in the superiority of the British system of cabinet government, was to weld the Democratic majority in Congress into an efficient, compact unit capable of driving his program through against any resistance.

To fuse the diverse elements of his party he depended on many techniques. He held frequent conferences with groups of congressional leaders both at the White House and in the President's room in the Capitol, which now saw more use than ever before in history. He put in a private telephone which connected him directly with the Senate. Presidential emissaries were everywhere on the Hill, and Burleson dangled fat plums before the dubious and the rebellious. Special presidential messages rained down on Congress. Through regular press conferences Wilson made sure that his "off the record" opinions received wide publicity. "His policy was to build up a strong *esprit de corps*," Ray Stannard Baker has written. Not only did he threaten the recalcitrant, he also rewarded the faithful. Harassed by his multitudinous obligations, he still found time to dash off charming notes to loyal supporters. "May I not express my warm admira-tion of the course you have taken?" he wrote Senator Ashurst, who had hewn to the administration line on the tariff in the face of strong pressure from his Arizona con-stituents. "It is not only in the highest degree manly, but it is most wise and public spirited."

When critics objected to his methods, calling him highhanded and dictatorial, he replied that such charges were absurd. He was not driving the congressmen, he was merely trying "to mediate their own thoughts and purposes." The Democratic members might be operat-ing with machine-like precision, but only because "they have found out that I am honest and that I have no per-sonal purpose of my own to serve." This, of course, was either naïveté, or hypocrisy, or self-delusion—probably the last.

Wilson called the reform program that he advocated in 1913 "The New Freedom." As Russel B. Nye, the historian of Middle-Western progressivism, has ob-served: " 'The New Freedom' . . . meant exactly what it said—the restoration of individual competition." To Wilson, the major social and economic problems of the age were the result of rapid industrialization and the growth of monopoly. Monopoly, the great evil, was merely the end product of something in itself desirable— competition. In the public interest, therefore, competi-tion should be restored by the destruction of the great monopolies, and maintained by outlawing the business practices that had led to monopoly in the first place.

In opposition to the Wilsonian approach, Theodore Roosevelt advocated his "New Nationalism," which faced the same problem (monopoly) with the same ob-jective (the public welfare), but which sought to apply

a different solution (*regulating* big business without destroying it). Roosevelt argued that industrial concentration was often both inevitable and useful; if its anti-social
practices could be curbed it need not be feared. Where
Wilson would break up the trusts and depend upon competition to protect the public, Roosevelt would set up a
government commission to protect the public by policing
big business without destroying its efficiency.

Neither concept was new. The idea of restoring competition was at least as old as the Sherman Anti-Trust
Act of 1890, while since 1887 the Interstate Commerce
Commission had possessed the power to regulate the
transportation industry in the public interest. Nor was
the practical distinction between the New Freedom and
the New Nationalism in any sense absolute. Roosevelt,
after all, was the first trust-buster. In 1912 Wilson said:
"I am not afraid of any corporation, no matter how big,"
and before he was finished he put his hand to many laws
that the New Nationalists had espoused. The two points
of view have not proved antithetical as practiced in the
United States, and both flourish in our own day. Still,
the names provide convenient labels for two approaches
to the problems of early twentieth-century reform.

It was natural that Wilson, with his original orienta-
tion toward *laissez-faire* economics, should adopt the
New Freedom philosophy as his compromise with progressivism. It required no essential change in his thinking,
merely an acceptance of the fact that nineteenth-century
conditions no longer existed and that only government
action could restore them. During the early stages of the
presidential campaign he fumbled vaguely with the basic
question of special privilege versus equal rights. But it
was not until he met Louis D. Brandeis that he was able
to work out his specific plans for reform.

Brandeis was a prominent progressive lawyer (some called him a radical) who had made a reputation by fighting railroad monopoly in New England and defending labor against exploitation all over the nation. Late in August 1912 he lunched with Wilson at the Governor's summer home in Sea Girt. Persuasively he argued for the idea of restoring competition and then protecting it by government regulation. Wilson was impressed. It was directly from Brandeis that he derived his plans for decentralizing the banking system and strengthening the Anti-Trust Law, the very core of the New Freedom.

Wilson's first step upon taking office was to call Congress into special session to consider lowering the duties on foreign imports. Tariff reduction was only indirectly related to the New Freedom philosophy, but it was a subject particularly congenial to Wilson. It was one topic on which he had not changed his views since becoming a politician, it was an ancient Democratic "issue," and it was popular in the South. The Republicans had bungled their own attempt at tariff revision under Taft, and the public clamor for lowering the schedules was loud and constantly increasing.

Wilson's tariff bill, which became the Underwood-Simmons Act of 1913, was the first significant reduction of duties since before the Civil War. Its passage was a tribute to his brilliant management of Congress and especially of public opinion. The difficulty with tariff legislation, as Taft and other presidents have discovered to their consternation, is that it is one area where party discipline is extremely hard to maintain. Local interests tend to predominate, and lobbying reaches a peak as the representatives of every conceivable product strive to justify the exclusion of foreign competitors.

Lobbying and logrolling had defeated Taft; they did

not stop Wilson. First he lashed out at the lobbyists. "Washington has seldom seen so numerous, so industrious, or so insidious a lobby," he announced. "It is of serious interest to the country that the people at large should have no lobby . . . while great bodies of astute men seek to create an artificial opinion and overcome the interests of the public for their private profit." The solution, he stated plainly, was for the people to lobby in their own behalf by deluging their representatives with expressions of their views. The public responded, and many a hesitant senator became a supporter of the Underwood-Simmons bill.

Wilson also pressured congressmen directly. The bill passed the House easily enough, but party discipline was harder to enforce in the Senate. Yet Wilson was able to bring about what the *New York Times* called "the first caucus of Democratic senators that anyone can remember" and persuade it to make the tariff bill a party measure. He held conferences, wrote letters, and made use of his new private line to the Hill. "Let me say that I fully recognize the difficulty of your position," he told one of the Louisiana senators who was under great local pressure to maintain the tariff on sugar. "You will, I am sure, understand me, however, if I say that the conclusion I, myself, draw from the circumstances is different from that which you evidently draw." After this polite introduction he read the senator a lecture on party loyalty— "those who have been overruled should accept the principle of party government." The fight went on interminably through the steaming-hot Washington summer, but on September 9, the bill passed substantially as Wilson had planned. A signal triumph, it increased Wilson's standing with the people, and what was of more practical importance at the moment, gave him firm control over his party in Congress.

As was his custom, Wilson pushed his advantage vigorously. Although many congressmen claimed to be exhausted, he insisted that they remain in Washington until they had acted on his banking reform plan. His foes groaned and (it may be supposed) swore—Senator Lodge was so incensed that he suffered a severe attack of ulcers—but Wilson persisted and in the end won out.

The need for overhauling the banking system was apparent to all. Under the Civil War National Banking Act the volume of paper money varied with the size of the national debt, and bore little relation to the changing needs of the economy. Money tended increasingly to pile up in the big Eastern commercial centers, while the rest of the nation suffered a currency "famine." All thoughtful students of the problem admitted the need for reform, but there was no agreement as to what should be done.

It was a great advantage to Wilson that he had no specific plan of his own. For without offending his conscience, he was able to mediate between the conservatives, who wished to maintain banker control over the currency, and the progressives, who wished the government to run the system and issue the money itself. At first he leaned toward the conservatives. He told Carter Glass, who led the administration forces in the House, that he was for "plenty of centralization, but not too much." But when the progressives flatly refused to go along with private control, he accepted their demands that the system be managed by a government commission (the Federal Reserve Board), and that the new currency be backed by the United States, though this

scarcely jibed with the New Freedom philosophy of individual competition. Once decided, however, he stood
by his guns against conservative counterarguments. It was
difficult to marshal public opinion in such a technical
field, but he cracked the party whip in Congress relent-
lessly. When Glass threatened to resign his post, discouraged by the petty haggling in his committee, Wilson
said to him: "Damn it, don't resign old fellow; outvote
them!" "Mac," he told Secretary of the Treasury Mc-
Adoo one hot summer day, "please say to the gentlemen on the Hill who urge a postponement of this matter
that Washington weather, especially in these days, fully
agrees with me and that unless final action is taken . . .
at this session I will immediately call Congress in extraordinary session. . . ." In the end it was not heat but
the Christmas spirit that caused the opposition to give in.
Wilson announced that there would be no holiday recess
unless a vote was taken. On December 19 there was a
vote, and the Federal Reserve Act became law shortly
thereafter.

However important in themselves Wilson's tariff and
banking legislation merely nibbled at the edges of a key
problem of the age, the monopolistic control of industry.
In his annual message of January 1914, he turned to this
basic issue. Again the congressional struggle was long-
drawn-out, and it was not until the autumn that the Clay-
ton Anti-Trust and Federal Trade Commission Acts received his signature.

In this fight Wilson showed less drive and decision
than in his first year. Should labor unions be exempted
from the anti-trust laws? The President seemed unable
to make up his mind. He was also torn between the
whole idea of trust-busting and the Rooseveltian principle of *regulating* business through a government com-

mission. After forcing the House to approve a strong anti-trust bill, he decided to concentrate instead on the creation of a Federal Trade Commission empowered to issue cease-and-desist orders in cases where competition was being smothered. Though both measures were eventually passed, the anti-trust bill was weakened by Senate amendments that Wilson had failed to oppose, and the new F.T.C. was hampered by the poor quality of the men Wilson appointed to it.

In part Wilson's faltering leadership reflected an unwillingness to antagonize business. He believed that most prominent industrialists were sincerely interested in cleaning their own houses. He was further deterred by the fact that the nation was suffering from a business slump in 1914.

But more important was the growing pressure of foreign problems on the President's time and thinking. When Wilson had consulted House about Cabinet appointments in the winter of 1912, the Colonel had suggested that the indispensable but supposedly inept Bryan be placed in charge of the State Department, because, as House put it: "Foreign affairs were dull." But since then the world, as House admitted, had turned "topsy-turvy." When Wilson signed the anti-monopoly bills Europe had already exploded into war. Though quite unaware of it, he was about to enter the climactic period of his life.

VI

ABOUT a month after Wilson's inauguration, Colonel House asked him if he had given any special instructions to the newly appointed Ambassador to Great Britain, Walter Hines Page. Wilson answered casually that he had not, but assumed that Page would be "diplomatic and conciliatory." This, he implied, was all that was required to conduct foreign relations successfully. It was not that he considered diplomacy unimportant. He made a great effort to obtain topflight men for all the ambassadorships. But (and in this he merely reflected an ancient American misconception) he believed that for America diplomacy was simple—politeness and good will were policy enough. With so many complex and pressing domestic problems to be faced, foreign affairs could be relegated to the background.

But Wilson was a victim of circumstances. By the time the Great War broke out in the summer of 1914 he was beginning to see the insufficiency of his well-meaning but cavalier "policy." Meanwhile he paid a high price in lost goals, misdirected efforts, and embarrassing inconsistencies.

Foreign problems were petty enough in the beginning. President Taft's unfortunately phrased "Dollar Diplomacy," which meant in essence imperialism based on financial influence rather than bayonets, offended Wilson's conception of national honor at the same time that it angered big-business-hating progressives. He ordered the State Department to withdraw its support of an international consortium of bankers who were negotiating a large loan to China, and immediately the American financiers withdrew. It was as simple as that.

However, in areas closer to home, the solutions were more complicated. In addition to Dollar Diplomacy, Wilson was particularly offended by "Big Stick" imperialism as practiced by Theodore Roosevelt in the Caribbean region. There must be no more selfish intervention in the affairs of Latin American nations, no more oppression of struggling peoples for the benefit of American investors. All nations, however weak, must be treated as equals; America's duty was to help rather than control her small neighbors to the south, assisting them in their strivings for prosperity and democracy. Arthur S. Link has called Wilson's policy "missionary diplomacy," and the term is apt, for it was moralistic, philanthropic, evangelical, and curiously ethnocentric and unrealistic. Just as the early Spanish friars had sought to impose Western Christianity on the primitive Indians, so Wilson tried to fashion their uneducated, poverty-stricken, dictator-ridden descendants in the image of middle-class New Jersey progressives and Nebraska farmers. He did not seem to realize that intervention for whatever motive was still intervention, and that to proud Latin Americans the "big brother" was almost as obnoxious as the greedy conqueror.

Secretary of State Bryan did not help the situation. As devoted as Wilson to the aims of missionary diplomacy, hard-working and benign, he was too provincial to handle Latin American problems wisely. Much unjustified abuse was directed at him by cynical and sophisticated men who resented his refusal to serve liquor at State Department functions, and who were embarrassed by his undignified appearances on the Chautauqua lecture circuit. In fact, such critics were merely expressing their own prejudices; Bryan was in many ways an excellent Secretary of State. But he injured the diplomatic service,

particularly in Latin America, by filling supposedly unimportant consulates with untrained and sometimes cor-
rupt political hacks (he called them "deserving Democrats"). And both he and Wilson failed totally to
understand the Latin American point of view. Their well-
intentioned but fumbling efforts to free countries like
Nicaragua, Haiti, and the Dominican Republic from the
control of American bankers only stirred up unrest and
factionalism. For the right reasons they often backed the
wrong elements, and the results were bloodshed, destruction, and, in the end, action for American marines. The
case of Mexico illustrates this bungling most clearly.

During the long and bitter Mexican crisis, a British
diplomat said to Wilson: "When I go back to England,
I shall be asked to explain your Mexican policy. Can
you tell me what it is?" The President replied with great
conviction: "I am going to teach the South American re-
publics to elect good men!"

The Mexican revolution was in full swing when Wilson became President, and it was following a classic pattern. A reform movement directed by moderates had
overthrown a tyrant only to be swamped in turn by the
forces of protest it had released. Labor leaders, agrarian
reformers, military despots, and common bandits were
soon engaged in a bloody struggle to control the country.
Shortly before Wilson's inauguration General Victoriano
Huerta had seized power by treacherously murdering the
incumbent president, but his rule was at once contested
by rival forces.

Wilson sympathized with the revolutionary movement as such. He was eager to help the struggling Mexican masses along the road to self-government and material well-being. He felt that the interests of Americans
in Mexico should be subordinated to the needs of the

Mexicans, even when this meant the destruction of American property and the loss of American lives. He pledged himself not to intervene; he urged "watchful waiting" while the Mexicans worked out their destiny in their own way. Yet he was too much the Presbyterian evangelist not to feel that he knew what was good for Mexico, and too much the professor to resist trying to teach the Mexican people what he knew.

Wilson realized that his policy would be unpopular with many Americans. The few whose interests were threatened in Mexico would be reinforced by the many whose belligerent patriotism would be roused by violations of American "rights." But he was not prepared for the Mexicans' own reaction to his well-meant "assistance." And, as had so often happened in the past, he developed distressing personal antagonisms that made it impossible for him to deal dispassionately with the real issues. He spoke in highflown phrases of international "sympathy and understanding," of exalting "morality" over "expediency," and "human rights" over "material interests," but he became so irritated by General Huerta that he allowed his feelings to dictate to his ideals.

Huerta, a stubborn, unscrupulous tyrant, was a type calculated to repel Wilson immediately. To recognize his callous seizure of power was unthinkable, despite the well-established international principle that recognition does not constitute approval. Instead Wilson denounced him, proclaimed to the world that he did not represent the Mexican people, and tried to persuade the major European powers to withdraw the routine recognition they had given him. These actions, though unorthodox, were perfectly sound. Huerta's rule was by no means secure; recognition could be denied on *de facto* grounds without seriously stretching the facts. But Wilson soon went beyond denunciation. He was barely dissuaded from sending Great Britain a dangerously strong note questioning her motives in recognizing Huerta, and he entered into negotiations with Huerta's Mexican enemies that would, if successful, have involved military intervention by the United States.

His detestation of Huerta undermined his resolution to let Mexico solve her own problems. It led him to idealize other Mexican leaders scarcely less odious than the tyrant himself. Even the bloodthirsty bandit, Pancho Villa, appeared "not so bad as he had been painted." Finally it led Wilson to the extraordinary step of making war on Huerta as an individual.

The pretext was an "insult" involving the arrest of a small party of American sailors by Mexican officials in the port of Tampico in April 1914. When a suitable apology was not forthcoming, Wilson ordered troops to occupy the city of Vera Cruz, making clear, however, that it was Huerta, not Mexico, that he was punishing. This rash act did not influence Huerta but it had a profound effect upon Wilson. For the landings were resisted, and lives were lost on both sides. Huerta's Mexican opponents denounced the invasion as loudly as any of his friends. The President's supposed intentions meant nothing to patriotic Mexicans; they were outraged by the presence of foreign soldiers on their soil.

Clearly Wilson had not expected resistance. His deepest sensibilities were horrified by the shedding of blood. He could not escape the devastating fact that by intervening he was doing exactly what his imperialistic American critics had wanted all along. Like an emotional flagwaver he seemed ready to fight a war with a weak neighbor over a mere diplomatic punctilio. When he appeared to answer the questions of excited Washington reporters his face was as pale as parchment, and he was visibly shaken by the enormity of the situation. Later the White House head usher noted him pacing up and down alone on the White House lawn, worried and uncertain over the possible results of his actions.

Fortunately, the day was saved by the timely offer of three South American nations to mediate the dispute. Wilson seized at the opportunity, and although the mediators settled nothing, time eased the crisis as Huerta's enemies finally drove him from power. Wilson gratefully recognized the authority of his successor, Venustiano Carranza. For a time American-Mexican relations were less tense. But when the European war broke out a few months later, the lesson of Vera Cruz loomed large in Wilson's mind. His whole neutrality policy reflected his awareness of the dangers involved in hasty action and ill-considered threats.

There was another long-range result of this unfortunate incident. It produced the first clash between the President and Senator Lodge of Massachusetts. Lodge was a partisan who distrusted all Democrats, but until the Vera Cruz crisis he had been remarkably tolerant of Wilson. He felt that the President was "extraordinarily green" in foreign relations, but that he was doing his best. In January 1914, during the Panama Canal Tolls dispute, Lodge had caused a stir by calling for bipartisan support of Wilson's policy of equal charges for all ships, and Wilson had written him a characteristic note of appreciation. But Lodge bristled when, at a meeting with congressional leaders, Wilson characterized the invasion of Mexico as an attack on Huerta personally. There was a sharp exchange, Lodge arguing that intervention should be based on "the true and international ground"—the protection of American life and property—and Wilson protesting that this would lead to war. The Senator, his lip curled in an aristocratic sneer, retorted that to him it looked like war in any event. Then, as events seemed about to bear Lodge's prediction out, Wilson vacillated and sought to back down, which only served to increase Lodge's contempt. "Wilson is very obstinate on political measures," Lodge wrote Theodore Roosevelt, "but . . . in foreign relations, he flinches."

In the Mexican crisis Wilson knew what he wanted to accomplish. But when the European war broke out, he, like most Americans, was caught in a maze of conflicting feelings. His instinctive reaction was to keep out of the fight. Intellectually he was far from certain as to which side was really the aggressor. It seemed obvious that American interests would best be served by remaining at peace. But emotionally his sympathies lay with England, France, and their allies. He told House that "if Germany won it would change the course of our civilization and make the United States a military nation," and he was horrified by the Germans' ruthless invasion of Belgium. The German philosophy, he said, was "essentially selfish and lacking in spirituality."

In this conflict between mind and heart Wilson was in the company of a large majority of the people, but unlike many of them he could not resolve the conflict easily in favor of his feelings. As always he dreaded having his actions influenced by his personal inclinations. He determined to be *really* neutral—even in thought—lest his sympathies prejudice his sense of right and wrong. With the iron will that characterized him whenever he saw something in terms of duty or morals, he insisted on impartiality. So thoroughly did he indoctrinate his own family that when one of his daughters happened to express admiration of the French people in their struggle with the invader she suddenly stopped, and asked, conscience-stricken: "Oh dear! Was that unneutral?"

Aside from the psychological impossibility of being neutral in thought, complete impartiality was unworkable, even for Wilson. Americans did not want to fight, but most of them wanted the Allies to win. When both belligerents, struggling for their very existence in the world's first total war, adopted policies that injured the United States, the nation looked differently upon Allied violations of its rights than upon those made by the Central Powers. England interrupted American trade with Germany, using her sea power in an attempt to starve her enemies into submission. She paid little heed to the rights of neutrals, instituting an "illegal" blockade and defining contraband so broadly as to outrage American exporters. For their part, the Germans loosed their deadly U-boats against Allied shipping, sending to the bottom millions of dollars' worth of American goods en route to Allied markets, and, far worse, killing American citizens in the act of exercising their undoubted right as neutrals to travel on the high seas in wartime. Logic would have impelled the United States to treat all violations alike; emotion required that a distinction be drawn.

It was easy to rationalize the distinction. England seized American goods—but paid for what she took. Germany destroyed goods without compensation. The English interfered with American property rights. The Germans killed American men, women, and children. Wilson's conscience resisted this easy solution to the national dilemma at the same time that his emotions welcomed it. As a result his policy was uncertain and contradictory.

In the beginning he tried to be completely impartial. He forbade officers of the armed forces even to discuss the war in public, and asked movie audiences to refrain from expressing approval of either side when war pictures were shown. He insisted that the U. S. Steel Corporation cancel a fifty-million-dollar order for submarine parts for the Allies, and refused to permit bankers to make loans to either side. He told Germany that she would be held to "strict accountability" for attacks on American shipping, and protested to England against her violations of neutral rights. He tried to force Congress to pass a law authorizing the government to purchase German ships that were hiding in American ports, even though the Allies had announced that they would not recognize the legality of such transfers of ownership. Indeed, the more extreme American friends of the Allies accused him of being pro-German. Of course, Wilson was never pro-German. The ship-purchase bill was designed to overcome the shortage of vessels in which to transport American goods overseas, and also to prevent the shortage-inspired profiteering of shipowners.

But with the passage of time his impartiality weakened. Though the Germans agreed to spare American ships, Wilson pushed them further by bringing up the question of injury to Americans traveling on Allied merchantmen. At the same time, his complaints about British policy grew less demanding. He conceded that there were "no very important questions of principle" involved in American protests against the British, that these were made merely for the record, and that Anglo-American claims and counterclaims could be thrashed out *after* the war. The ban on private loans was also lifted, and America soon became a major source of munitions for the Allies. Yet Wilson remained troubled in his own mind.

Probably a clear-cut policy of either friendliness for the Allies or rigid neutrality would have been better. Ambassador Page, for example, was wholeheartedly for the Allied cause. He advised close co-operation with Great Britain and frankly condemned "German militarism." To have followed his advice would have led the United States into the war much sooner, but it probably would have reduced the loss of life and property for all the belligerents. Wilson, however, rejected Page's position. "Walter Page," he wrote, "is undoubtedly too much affected by the English view of things and needs a bath in American opinion." This was true enough, but Wilson also rejected the stand of a really neutral adviser like William Jennings Bryan. Bryan was not pro-German, but he believed that German violations of neutral rights were not essentially different from Allied violations. He thought that the United States could force both sides to obey international law by threatening to cut off the flow of vital American supplies. Such a policy, if adopted, would probably have kept America out of the war, but it might well have meant that Germany would eventually have triumphed. Wilson was certainly influenced by Bryan's arguments, but, unlike his Secretary of State, he could not accept the possibility of German victory. So he steered a course midway between the desires of Page and Bryan. Perhaps public opinion, equally distraught, forced him to this inconsistency, but Wilson himself, unable to resolve the problem in his own mind, did little to guide public feeling toward an intelligent course.

Nowhere was Wilson's uncertainty more debilitating than in his approach to the question of building up the nation's armed strength. In the beginning he made the mistake of equating the desire to remain at peace with a refusal to develop a powerful military machine. He fell into this error largely because of the general belief that the United States could not conceivably go to war against

the Allies. This being so, he felt that any expansion of
the armed forces must be interpreted as an act unfriendly
to the Central Powers, and when advisers suggested that
a large army might be necessary merely as a protection in
the post-war world, he scoffed, arguing that no matter
who won the war all the contestants would be completely exhausted. He resisted all pressure for increasing
the 1915 military budget, telling Congress it must not
"turn America into a military camp" or require American youths "to spend the best years of their lives making
soldiers of themselves."

Even as a means of remaining neutral this policy
proved shortsighted, for American military weakness actually encouraged the Germans to take actions that forced
the United States into the fight. As early as the summer
of 1915 the American Ambassador in Berlin complained: "The people here are firmly convinced that we
can be slapped, insulted, and murdered with absolute
impunity," and Colonel House was saying: "If war
comes . . . it will be because we are totally unprepared
and Germany feels that we are impotent."

Such warnings were brought home to Wilson by the
torpedoing of the British liner, Lusitania, in May 1915.
Many Americans went down with the Lusitania, Wilson
protested vigorously, and for a time war with Germany
seemed likely. But the futility and the danger of chal-
lenging the Germans while the United States was practically unarmed now became apparent. If American neutral rights were to be respected, they must be backed up
by more than words.

Wilson, however, was tortured by the complications
of the situation, and moved slowly. Outraged by the
sinking of the Lusitania, the interventionist elements in
America redoubled their clamor for increased armaments

and at the same time demanded that we join the fight at the side of the Allies. Wilson did not want to associate preparedness with war in this way. Further, he may have realized that his own emotional commitment to the Allies was in part responsible for the *Lusitania* crisis. If he had been strictly impartial in dealing with violations of American rights, armed merchantmen would never have been allowed to leave American ports and the submarines would perhaps have followed the recognized procedure of visit and search. If he had accepted the not wholly unreasonable suggestion of the Germans that Americans stay off munitions-laden liners like the *Lusitania*, no United States citizens would have been killed in the disaster. Finally, although he had progressed to the belief that military expansion was necessary, whether as a prelude to joining the Allies or as a means of preserving neutrality, he hesitated to initiate a program of preparedness without determining which of these alternatives would be the result.

For months he delayed, but at last the imperatives of the situation forced him to act. He made his first public appeal for a military build-up at a dinner at the Manhattan Club of New York in November 1915. A crack reporter, sitting a few feet from the speakers' table, has left us a vivid impression of the President's disquietude. During the meal he was glum, scarcely exchanging a word with his companions. When he rose to speak his unhappy face dampened the applause, and his words were strained and unnatural. As he called for increased armaments in the name of national defense, some of the old Wilson magic came through, but only for a moment. "He was taking his medicine without licking the spoon, and it was a bitter dose," the reporter noted.

Even after committing himself, Wilson could not enter wholeheartedly into the preparedness program. It is true that he carried his appeal to the people in a series of effective speeches throughout the Middle West, but otherwise his customary forceful leadership was entirely lacking. His indecisiveness showed up in his refusal to back the vigorous program of expansion outlined by Secretary of War Garrison, even though his action resulted in Garrison's resignation. He did finally maneuver the preparedness legislation through Congress, but he got much less than he had originally asked for. Considering the strong pacifist sentiment in Congress, particularly among the Democrats, it is not surprising that he failed to get more; what is surprising is that he did not fight harder. Had his "duty" been clearer to him, he unquestionably would have done so, whatever the odds.

There is another factor that may help explain Wilson's faltering over preparedness, and indeed over the whole problem of neutrality in 1914 and 1915. Throughout the period he was emotionally undone, first by the death of Ellen Wilson, and then by his courtship of Edith Bolling Galt, whom he married in December 1915. Ellen had never been strong, and her life as first lady overtaxed her. In 1914 it was apparent to everyone but Wilson that she was failing. By the summer her condition was hopeless, and on August 6, she died.

For a man so dependent upon family love for relaxation and personal security the blow was crippling. "Of course you know what has happened to me," he wrote a friend on August 7, "but I wanted you to know direct from me. God has stricken me almost beyond what I can bear." For days he was deeply distraught, inconsolable. A friend watched him reading some of the letters of condolence that poured in, his lips quivering, his eyes filled with tears. "If you could have been with him," this ob-

server wrote, "you too would be overcome. I never have
seen such real genuine grief."

He quickly forced himself to attend to the public business, and soon seemed in command of his sorrow. Ray
Stannard Baker interviewed him in September and noted:
"He looked very well—clear-eyed, confident, cheer-
ful—a neat gray suit looking as though it were just from
the tailor—a black band on his left arm, a dark tie with
a gold ornament. His desk was extremely neat, with a
bouquet of roses upon it. He was affable and frank." This
was but an outward glimpse, however. The problems of
his office helped to occupy his mind, Wilson confessed,
"but, Oh! how hard, how desperately hard, it has been
to face them, and to face them worthily! Every night
finds me exhausted,—dead in heart and body, weighed
down with a leaden indifference and despair."

His character suffered as well as his feelings. Ellen
Wilson had, as ex-President Taft noted, served as "an
antidote" to her husband's "somewhat angular disregard
of other people's feelings." After her death he became
even less tolerant than formerly of those who disagreed
with him. He began to have trouble with his Cabinet,
and to grow somewhat irascible.

For any man the loss of a dearly loved wife is a tragedy. For Woodrow Wilson, who needed female com-
panionship so badly, the tragedy was especially deep.
Yet, paradoxically, the severity of his loss led him to a
quick remarriage.

One March day in 1915, Helen Bones, a cousin of
Wilson's who was living in the White House, went
walking in Rock Creek Park with her good friend Edith
Bolling Galt, the widow of a Washington jeweler. On
such occasions they usually took tea afterward at Mrs.
Galt's residence, but this time Miss Bones insisted that

they go to the White House, since she thought Wilson was out playing golf and would not be disturbed by them. But as they entered, they ran into the President and his physician, Dr. Cary Grayson. Introductions were exchanged, and it was decided that they would all have tea together in the Oval Room. Mrs. Galt was charming. Wilson saw a gracious, good-looking woman in her early forties, radiant with vitality. Her speech and manner reflected her old Virginia background; she could trace her ancestry, he soon learned with pleasure, back to John Rolfe and Pocahontas. The President was fascinated. Twice he even laughed heartily at something she said. Miss Bones seemed to feel the very atmosphere about him change. "I can't say that I foresaw in that first minute what was going to happen," she confided later to a relative. "It may have taken ten minutes—"

Soon Wilson was accompanying the ladies on drives, and Mrs. Galt was dining at the White House. He began to send her flowers, and books that he thought would interest her (Wordsworth's poems, and even Bagehot and Burke!), borrowing them from the Library of Congress when they were not readily available at the bookstores.

He carried on a whirlwind courtship under incredible difficulties. It was almost impossible, because of his position, to have Mrs. Galt to himself. Always they must be chaperoned—to say nothing of the inevitable secret service men who were never out of sight. But Wilson persevered, for after meeting her he was a new man. The tenseness and strain had evaporated from his face; his depression was gone. "She seemed to come into our life here like a special gift from Heaven," he explained in wonder. By April he was writing her arch *billets-doux:* "If it rains this evening would it be any fun for you to

come around and have a little readin? If it does *not* rain,
are you game for another ride?" In the comparative privacy of the White House he told her of his boyhood, and
of Father Joseph's educational methods. On May 3 he
proposed. She put him off at first, but by September he
had won her.

Impetuously, he insisted on a speedy union. His political advisers quaked at the thought of marriage before the
1916 election. For the President to take a new wife so
soon after the death of Ellen Wilson might appear shock-
ing to many voters. But no one was willing to bell the
cat. Postmaster General Burleson nominated Secretary
of the Navy Daniels, but Daniels declined what he called
"the difficult, and, perhaps, dangerous position of Minister Plenipotentiary to the Court of Cupid." Faithful
Joe Tumulty finally brought the subject up (to the everlasting resentment of Mrs. Galt,) but Wilson was inflexible. "If the people do not trust me," he said, "now is the
time to find out."

So they were married on schedule. The ugly rumors
anticipated by the politicians did not fail to appear, and
some people professed to be scandalized. "My wife is
dead!" Theodore Roosevelt sneered. "Long live my
wife!" But Wilson did not mind—or better, was too
happy to be hurt. His appraisal of the public reaction to
his marriage proved to be generally correct. It was certainly not an important issue in the 1916 campaign. But
his interest in his bride may well have contributed to his
relative ineffectiveness in the preparedness fight in Congress.

Still, Congress did pass legislation strengthening the
armed forces in the spring of 1916. In May of that year,
after Wilson's sharp protest over the sinking of the chan-
nel steamer, *Sussex*, Germany finally agreed to stop sub-

marine attacks on merchantmen. At least for the moment it seemed that Wilson had conquered his uncertainties. Bryan, disturbed by the President's stand on the U-boat issue, had resigned in June 1915 and was replaced by Robert Lansing, who favored a policy of friendliness toward the Allies. The swelling flood of orders for war materials was binding the United States closer and closer to the Allied cause. The country seemed ready, if not for war, at least for a policy of rationalized neutrality frankly favoring England and France.

But Wilson was not ready. Having pressed Germany far more closely than England until Germany gave in, he now turned upon British violations of American rights with a sharpness absent in earlier months. It was as though, having permitted his pro-British feelings to go a certain distance, he now reared back in alarm and became more strictly neutral. The conflict between his mind and his heart was as strong as ever, and consequently American policy continued to vacillate.

British policies in 1916 did not ease the situation. Intensifying their economic warfare, the British began opening American mail, forbade their people to transact business with a long list of American firms suspected of trading with the Germans, and sought in other ways to control neutral commerce. The vigorous suppression of an Irish rebellion also caused indignation in the United States, where a large and vocal Irish-American population was already hostile to the British.

In anger, Wilson sought and obtained retaliatory legislation against "the blacklist" and prepared a note "as sharp and final as the one to Germany on the submarines." The British, he told House, were "poor boobs!" When Ambassador Page returned from London for a visit, the President refused to see him for weeks, and then cut his friend deeply by his comments on British perfidy. Yet he could not bring himself to *act* against the Allies. The retaliatory legislation was never used. "What would happen if no nation stood ready to assist the world with its finances and to supply it with its food?" Wilson asked. "There is a moral obligation laid on us to keep free the courses of our commerce." Though his remarks were phrased in general terms, he was acutely aware that the preponderance of American money and goods was going to the Allies.

Thus matters drifted uncertainly through the dismal fall and winter of 1916, while two great armies locked in bloody stalemate and hatreds mounted. Across the Atlantic, the neutral United States viewed both sides darkly, and turned its thoughts to a presidential election.

VII

THE VEXATIONS of neutrality were enough to test the intelligence and patience of any man, yet in 1916 Wilson had also to face the problem of re-election. A Republican split had elected him in 1912. By 1916 there were signs that this split was being mended, and no Democrat since Grover Cleveland had beaten a united Republican Party. Wilson simply had to attract voters who had supported other candidates in 1912, and it soon became clear that his best chance lay in wooing the Progressives. In doing so Wilson laid himself open to the charge that he was unprincipled, just as he had at the time of his original "conversion" to progressivism in 1910.

His inconsistencies are easily demonstrated. In January 1916 he nominated his friend Brandeis for the Supreme Court. (In 1913 he had allowed himself to be persuaded that Brandeis was too "radical" even for the Cabinet.) In July he signed the Farm Loan Act, creating federal land banks to help ease rural credit. (Three years earlier he had said: "I have a very deep conviction that it is unwise and unjustifiable to extend the credit of the Government to a single class of the community"; now he argued that the law would "introduce business methods into farm finance.") In September he gave his approval to a federal child labor law. (While president of Princeton he had written that national child labor legislation was unconstitutional, based in theory on an "obviously absurd" interpretation of the commerce clause, and in 1914 he told Tumulty: "No child labor law yet proposed has seemed to me constitutional.") Wilson also pushed the Adamson Act through Congress, establishing an eight-hour day for railroad workers by federal edict, and showed signs of weakening his lifelong opposition to the protective tariff. By the fall of 1916 the Democrats had enacted almost every important plank in the Progressive platform of 1912.

Without denying that Wilson was aware of the political advantages of these actions, it would still be unfair to charge him with insincerity. He had cast off his penchant for doctrinaire philosophizing even before he entered politics, but in 1912 he was naturally inclined to keep as close to his original *laissez-faire* theories as possible; hence, for example, his stand in favor of restoring competition. The New Freedom's emphasis on individualism was also strengthened by Wilson's understandable wish to be different from Roosevelt, who was extolling the efficiency of the large corporations and the virtues of a powerful, centralized government. But experience in the White House was broadening; practical problems resisted simple solutions. Even Brandeis, who contributed so much to the New Freedom philosophy, was partially converted to the idea of a regulatory state.

More direct and positive federal legislation was also an outgrowth of the recurring crises of the neutrality period. The economic dislocations resulting from the war made impractical the New Freedom type of reform by indirection. Wilson supported the Adamson Act, for example, only after he had worked desperately for a private solution of a threatened railroad strike that would have crippled the economy. He urged the workers and the operators to settle their disputes by negotiation, and when the operators proved adamant, he begged them in the name of humanity and the national defense to accept a compromise. Only when they refused again did he say: "I pray God to forgive you, I never can," and call upon Congress to settle the issue.

Finally, Wilson's whole character made hypocrisy impossible for him. His faith in himself (some would call it egotism) and his sense of dedication to moral absolutes precluded at least conscious political trimming. The man who would not postpone his marriage to win votes, who pursued a plainly unpopular course in Mexico for an ideal, who refused to appeal to national prejudices at a time when flag-waving promised to pay big dividends, can scarcely be accused of insincerity merely because he violated a few abstract and, in the American experience, essentially meaningless theories of government, even if it is clear that he benefited thereby at the polls.

The President's intellectual honesty was put to a severe test during the campaign by the enthusiastic efforts of his supporters to capitalize on the success of his anti-submarine policy. The profound desire of the people to keep out of the war burst upon the politicians unexpectedly during the Democratic convention when the keynote speaker, Martin H. Glynn, casually referred to previous examples in American history in which diplomatic negotiation had avoided conflicts. The audience cheered, and Glynn picked up the cue and turned his speech into a paean of pacifism. The next day another orator reminded the delegates that without the loss of a single American life Wilson had "wrung from the most militant spirit that ever brooded above a battlefield an acknowledgment of American rights and an agreement to American demands," and the convention demonstrated wildly for more than twenty minutes. Thus was born the slogan: "He kept us out of war."

But Wilson would not press this specious argument. He could not deny that he had avoided involvement, for it was true. Yet the implications of the slogan distressed him. "I can't keep the country out of war," he complained to Josephus Daniels. "They talk of me as though I were a god. Any little German lieutenant can put us into the war at any time by some calculated outrage." Further, when some of his supporters tried to win over pro-German groups by means of the slogan, the President disowned them. The Republican candidate, Charles Evans Hughes, was at least willing to confer with the leaders of these elements, but Wilson treated them with icy contempt. When one Irish-American extremist sent him an impudent telegram, he replied: "I would feel deeply mortified to have you or anybody like you vote for me. Since you have access to many disloyal Americans and I have not, I will ask you to convey this message to them." This was not the statement of a man without principles.

Yet during the campaign Wilson was guilty of something worse than inconsistency. It was a small matter, but important for the light it sheds upon his personality, and for the role it played in his growing feud with Henry Cabot Lodge.

At the time of the *Lusitania* affair Wilson had prepared a stiff note of protest to Germany. Secretary Bryan, fearing a diplomatic break, had objected, and at his urging Wilson had written a "tip," or unofficial news release, to the effect that "administration circles" expected that the Germans would not be offended by the note, and that the whole issue could be settled amicably through negotiation. This statement would have taken most of the sting from the note itself, but it was never issued because certain of Wilson's advisers persuaded him to withhold it. The whole incident reflects Wilson's basic uncertainty about neutrality.

Of course, the public did not know about the "tip" at the time. But in October 1916, Senator Lodge obtained a slightly garbled version of the story. As he was informed, the modifying statement had been written as a "postscript" to the note itself. It had not been sent, only because members of the Cabinet had threatened to resign if it were. When Lodge released his account it caused a furor that was only stilled when Wilson issued a flat denial. "No postscript or amendment of the *Lusitania* note was ever written," he announced. It had been "suggested" that he tell the Germans that a proposal for arbitration would be acceptable, but, said the President, "I rejected the suggestion." This was literally true, but utterly false in spirit. Wilson had grasped at a minor inaccuracy in Lodge's account, and by implication asserted that the whole story was untrue.

Lodge knew enough of the details to realize that Wilson was equivocating, but he could prove nothing. "The President of United States has denied that there was any postscript to the *Lusitania* note and we are all bound, of course, to accept the President's denial just as he makes it," the Senator announced acidly. His already strong contempt for the President was further strengthened, while Wilson's hatred of Lodge became so bitter that he refused even to speak on the same platform with him.

The intensity of Wilson's reaction shows that he was transferring his own guilt-feelings to Lodge. The same sensitivity to personal criticism that led him to untruthfulness in the Princeton graduate-school fight was clearly at work here, as it was to be on other occasions in the future. It was derived, essentially, from the same flaw that made him a poor teacher of a seminar despite his incomparable talents in the lecture hall, the same quirk that made it almost impossible for him either to dismiss a disloyal subordinate or to trust a loyal adviser who expressed disagreement with one of his decisions. It re-

flected, of course, some inner insecurity, not a base nature. It calls more for sympathy than for condemnation.

Fortunately this side of Wilson did not show itself
when really large issues were at stake. It was apparent to
all that the 1916 election would be extremely close.
Sensing the possibility of defeat, Wilson was ready,
should he lose, to appoint Hughes Secretary of State and
then resign in his favor so that the nation would be
spared an "interregnum" in such critical times.[1] When,
on election night, early returns seemed to indicate a
Hughes sweep, the President was unperturbed. To Tumulty, who reported discouraging news over the telephone,
he said good-naturedly: "Well, Tumulty, it begins to
look as if we were badly licked. . . . The only thing I
am sorry for, and that cuts me to the quick, is that the
people apparently misunderstood us." He discussed the
matter coolly with members of his family until half past
ten, and then had a glass of milk and went to bed. "I
might stay longer," he remarked whimsically, "but you
are all so blue."

Late returns from the West swung the balance back
in his favor, and after agonizing days of uncertainty, his
re-election was assured. The issues of peace and progressivism seem to have given him his majority.

Cheered by this expression of public faith, Wilson determined to make a great effort to end the war by mediation. As the battles dragged on indecisively, the loss of
life and property constantly mounting, it seemed to Wilson that the greatest service he could render America and
the world would be to arbitrate between the hate-mad-
dened belligerents, and work for a settlement that would

[1] The plan called also for the resignation of Vice-President
Marshall.

prevent a recurrence of such senseless conflict. He was also acutely aware of the temper of his own people as expressed during the campaign. They wanted to remain at peace. Yet with both belligerents straining desperately to break the long deadlock on the battlefields, America might be forced toward war at any moment. What if Germany were to resume her attacks on unarmed ships? "I do not believe the American people would wish to go to war no matter how many Americans were lost at sea," he confessed unhappily to House. A crusade for peace seemed the only alternative to national disgrace.

The idea of acting as an arbitrator was not a new one for the President. "America," he had said the day the war broke out, "stands ready with calmness of thought and steadiness of purpose to help the rest of the world." But his sympathy for the Allies made it impossible for him to do much in the early stages of the struggle. The first mighty surge of the Germans across Belgium and France gave them the advantage. Peace at that time would have been possible only on terms disadvantageous to the Allies, and though Bryan urged him to act, Wilson held off.

Finally, in January 1915, he sent Colonel House to Europe for talks with English, French, and German leaders, but what little progress the Colonel made was wiped out by the torpedoing of the *Lusitania*. In that angry atmosphere, the United States was obviously unfit to mediate.

Wilson made another effort the following winter, but his own purposes were so unclear to him that it could not possibly have been effective. This time Colonel House suggested that Wilson propose a peace based on a return to conditions as of August 1914. The British had indicated to him that such a peace would be acceptable if it were backed by an American promise to join in guaranteeing it in the future. Surely Germany could not refuse such terms, but if she did, House argued, the United States should enter the war on the side of the Allies and force her to do so.

House used his great powers of persuasion and his keen insight into Wilson's character to the full. He portrayed a new and better world, a world perpetually at peace under the benign control of a powerful league of nations. "This is the part I think you are destined to play in this world tragedy," he explained. "It is the noblest part that has ever come to a son of man." Such an appeal was hard for Wilson to resist. With the submarine question still unsettled, the danger of trouble with Germany was acute in any case. Here was an opportunity either to prevent a break or to place it, if it came, upon the highest moral grounds. But he would not commit the nation irretrievably. He authorized House to say that the United States would "*probably*" intervene if Germany refused a fair peace. The Allied leaders, aware of the constitutional limitations on Wilson's freedom of action in declaring war, and sensing also his personal hesitation, were unwilling to accept so tenuous a promise. They offered House vague encouragement, but he returned to America convinced that both sides preferred another summer of fighting to a negotiated peace.

In a sense these talks could scarcely be called an attempt at mediation. House's suggestion, in effect, was to say to England and France: "If you cannot defeat Germany, we will try to persuade her to accept a draw; if that fails, we will join you in overwhelming her." But Wilson's ambivalence weakened the force of House's proposal; he was himself neither wholly neutral nor wholly pro-Allies. However, the events of 1916 altered the situation drastically. The *Sussex* pledge lessened the

submarine danger; the British blacklist undermined
American faith in British intentions; the election campaign revealed the depth of the people's desire for peace.
At last Wilson was ready to make a real effort to end the
war.

Soon after the election he plunged into the preparation of a note to the belligerents. His health was poor,
but he labored on, surrounded by documents, newspaper
clippings, and copies of speeches. The plan, he told his
anxious wife, might "prove the greatest piece of work of
my life." On November 27 he explained it to Colonel
House. The war was disturbing the civilization of the entire world; neutral nations along with the belligerents
were suffering deeply. While each side professed to be
interested in a just and lasting peace and denied any wish
to crush its foes, neither had ever defined the practical
objectives it was fighting for. Whatever these objectives
might be, unless the fighting were halted—and soon—all
might be so exhausted that it would be "too late to realize
the hopes which all men who love peace and justice en-
tertain." Both sides, therefore, should state "the terms
upon which a settlement . . . may be expected." Future American policy would depend upon what these
terms were.

Both House and Secretary of State Lansing felt that
the note was *too* neutral. Lansing argued that it would
offend the Allies, and, if Germany responded favorably
and the Allies did not, it could embroil the United States
in the war on the wrong side. House complained privately that Wilson had lost his grasp of the situation.
With characteristic indirectness he suggested reviving
the plan developed on his last trip to Europe. But Wilson replied: "We cannot go back to those old plans. We
must shape new ones," and he stated flatly that for the

United States, "there will be no war." He did agree to
modify his note before dispatching it, removing, for example, the veiled threat that American policy would be
shaped by the nature of the aims outlined by the belligerents. He did not, however, depart from the position of
true neutrality. The note, sent on December 18, created
a furor, but failed to achieve its purpose. The Allies were
offended by his cool declaration that both sides seemed
to be fighting for the same reasons and with the same
general aims. Neither side would reveal its objectives,
for the brutal truth was that each still sought to benefit
from the war. Having expended so much, neither was
willing to admit that all had been in vain.

Wilson was disappointed but he did not give up. On
January 22, 1917 he delivered his famous "peace without victory" speech before the Senate. A settlement im-
posed by a victor would settle nothing, he said. It could
not be permanent. It would breed hatred, and more wars.
Only a peace of "equality and a common participation in
a common benefit" could endure.

It was a desperate speech and characteristically an appeal over the heads of the European authorities to the
people themselves. "The real people I was speaking to
was neither the Senate nor foreign governments . . .
but the *people* of the countries now at war," he said
later. He was also speaking to his own people, for he
stressed America's responsibility to join in guaranteeing
the peace by taking part in a world organization strong
enough to enforce it.

Like the December note, this moving attempt was
doomed to failure. Before it was even written, the Germans, staking everything on the hope of quick military
victory, had decided to resume unrestricted submarine
warfare. On January 31 the German Ambassador in-

formed Secretary of State Lansing that even neutral ships would be attacked on sight. Three days later diplomatic relations with Germany were severed.

There followed two months of confusion and mounting tension. It had taken Wilson a long time to decide that the war was being fought for no good purpose, and he could not abandon this conclusion easily. Lansing urged him to declare war at once. War, he retorted, would settle nothing. The Secretary said the United States would be disgraced "if we failed to act." Wilson answered that he "would bear all the criticism and abuse" himself if the general welfare would be served thereby. House added his voice to Lansing's, and the other members of the Cabinet did so too. Someone asked the President which side he wanted to see win. Neither, he answered bitterly.

When he broke relations with Germany he stated specifically that this did not mean war. He refused to convoy American merchantment, or to ask Congress to arm them, until he learned, late in February, that Germany was intriguing to get Mexico and Japan to attack the United States. On March 18 U-boats sank three American ships. Again Lansing urged war, but still the President held back. "I felt that he was resisting the irresistible logic of events," Lansing recorded.

He could not resist much longer. On March 20 he met with his Cabinet. Every member counseled war. Burleson began to read telegrams showing that the people would support a declaration. "We are not governed by public feeling," Wilson declared. "I want to do right whether it is popular or not." But by the time the meeting was over he had given in. He did not announce a decision, but the next day he began to work on his war message.

Once decided, he did not turn back, but he suffered dreadful self-doubt. He lost sleep, appeared gray and drawn. Desperately he sought to convince himself that to fight was not merely necessary but also right. Had his interpretation of the war, resolved so recently and at such cost in anguished thought, been wrong? Had his original, instinctive feeling for the Allied cause been correct? If so, how to justify to his conscience the years of equivocation and delay? Could it be that the interventionists —could it be that even the hated Lodge—had all along been right, and he, Woodrow Wilson, wrong? A few hours before he finally spoke he told a trusted friend that he was still more uncertain about his course than he had ever been about anything.

But his uncertainty was not apparent when he appeared before Congress on the evening of April 2. Washington, its streets jammed, its buildings bedecked with flags, was tense with expectation. (That morning, Senator Lodge, aged sixty-six, had punched a pacifist in the jaw in the corridor of the Senate Office Building.) At eight thirty Wilson stood before packed galleries in the chamber of the House of Representatives. He spoke carefully and without gestures. The audience was hushed.

He assailed the German government for its resumption of submarine warfare. It was guilty of a "reckless lack of compassion or of principle," of "throwing to the winds all scruples of humanity," of "wanton and wholesale destruction of the lives of noncombatants," of "warfare against mankind." The nation must "accept the status of belligerent which has thus been thrust upon it." But the object must be "peace and justice," not conquest. "The world," (including Germany itself!) "must be made safe for democracy."

Thus Wilson fused his idea of peace without victory with the idea that Germany was the villain of the contest. This involved arguing that the German people were neither responsible for nor agreeable to the actions of their leaders—a most dubious assumption—and that the Allies would be as altruistic as Wilson himself when the day of victory arrived. But in the excitement of the moment few stopped to consider the full meaning of his words.

The nation responded enthusiastically, partisanship washed away on a wave of patriotism. As he left the hall to the cheers of the assembled dignitaries, even Lodge wrung his hand with enthusiasm. "Mr. President," the Senator said, "you have expressed in the loftiest manner possible the sentiments of the American people." Only after several weeks had passed did Lodge appreciate the implications of the message. Then he said to Theodore Roosevelt: "If that message was right, everything he has done for two years and a half is fundamentally wrong." But by then Wilson's past actions were of only academic interest. Congress had responded to his appeal quickly and with overwhelming majorities. By April 7 the United States was at war.

As Thomas A. Bailey has so aptly said, it is one of the great ironies of our history that "the peace-loving President Wilson . . . attained far greater success in making war than in making peace." Having expressed his fateful decision, he cast off most of the doubts that had shackled him during the years of neutrality and reasserted himself as a forceful leader. War produced a new situation with new problems, and Wilson responded brilliantly to the challenge. His ability to communicate his high aspirations to the masses served to unite the people when unity was most essential. His efficiency and de-

cisiveness helped to loose the bonds of custom that restricted the swift conversion of the economy from peace
to war. His comprehension of the tasks involved in producing, transporting, and using effectively America's
contribution to the defeat of the Central Powers was almost as important in the final victory as the thousands of
well-equipped troops whose guns and courage actually
won it.

Never had a President faced so many complicated
problems, all requiring rapid handling. It is true that
some of the difficulties were of his own making, out-
growths of his refusal to face realities between August
1914 and April 1917. For example, more effective leadership in the preparedness controversy would have prevented the costly delays in readying the army for battle
—six months need not have passed before the first draft-
ees reported for training. But much of the build-up could
not have been accomplished earlier. The financing of our
nearly bankrupt allies, the construction of a fleet of merchantmen to carry men and arms to the battlefields and
to replace the huge tonnages destroyed by submarines,
the allocation of scarce goods, the reorganization of the
war-strained railroad network, the encouragement of increased production of foodstuffs, and dozens of other
tasks could only be faced after we entered the fight. Wilson faced them all with confidence and energy.

Gradually, during the first year, he developed an organization for handling the emergency. He wisely decided not to burden the peacetime Departments with additional duties. Instead he created new boards to deal
with wartime problems. Thus the Committee on Public
Information, headed by George Creel, and the War In-
dustries Board, headed by Bernard Baruch, were set up.
Herbert Hoover was named Food Administrator, and

Harry Garfield Fuel Administrator. These men, along with Daniels of the Navy Department, Newton D. Baker of the War Department, McAdoo of the Treasury, and one or two others, became known as the "War Cabinet" and met weekly with the President to thrash out policy.

The meetings were held in Wilson's study, overlooking the Potomac. After greeting his advisers, passing out cigars, and perhaps telling a funny story to break the tension, the President would clear his desk and get down to work. Each member would raise his own particular problems, which all would discuss. Wilson served as coordinator; he kept the discussion orderly, absorbed information, and in the end made the decisions. These meetings were very time-consuming, and often the discussions seemed fruitless, but they were indispensable for Wilson and for the proper conduct of affairs. With each individual absorbed in his own particular field, only Wilson could maintain the broad perspective necessary when scarce materials had to be allocated and conflicting policies reconciled.

In all things he retained the power of decision, and accepted the responsibility that went with it. His grasp of details continually amazed his aides: "He showed . . . remarkable knowledge of our business problems." "He had his hand on the pulse of each Department." "His knowledge of things, his collection of ideas, his impressions of people, were astonishing in depth and variety." Even in military and naval affairs he played an intimate role, although in these technical fields he naturally leaned more heavily on others. Secretary Daniels has presented in his memoirs a long list of important military decisions made directly by Wilson. "I am an amateur," he would always begin, and then go on to offer his suggestions.

In addition to the burdens of administration, Wilson faced heavy legislative duties. Demonstrating once again his effectiveness as a "prime minister," Wilson pushed a great mass of novel, and therefore controversial, legislation through the Congress. Speed was essential, but though politics was supposedly "adjourned" for the duration, the nature of the decisions being made provoked lengthy debate.

With the Selective Service Act, for example, time was precious, yet many members of his own party were dead-set against the draft. Speaker Clark, majority leader Kitchin, and the chairman of the House Millitary Affairs Committee were all opposed. But Wilson pushed it through, making free use of Republican help (he even consulted Lodge upon occasion). He had the necessary draft-registration forms printed while the bill was still in debate so that it could be implemented quickly when passed. Though an aroused public opinion aided him greatly, the passage of the bill only six weeks after its introduction was a major personal triumph.

Such labors would have tested the endurance of a man of thirty, and Wilson was middle-aged, delicate, and already worn down by four years in the White House. He survived them because of his iron will and sense of duty, and because he used what strength he had with great efficiency, resting completely when it was possible to rest at all.

In wartime he was normally at his desk by six o'clock. Mrs. Wilson was usually with him, handing him routine papers for signing, blotting and removing them as he affixed his name to each. Actually, her services were far from being devoted to mere routine. Edith Wilson was a forceful personality as well as a charming woman. After her first husband's death, for example, she had taken over his jewelry business and run it with great competence. She sensed the influence she could exercise over the doting President, and never hesitated to use it, though always in a manner calculated to advance what she conceived to be his interests and the nation's. Their marriage marked the beginning (scarcely noticeable at the time) of Colonel House's eclipse, and also of Tumulty's. She was with Wilson almost constantly. She accompanied him on trips and on speaking tours; she even became his partner on the golf course. After America entered the war, her services were of incalculable value to him, physically, intellectually, and psychologically.

Mrs. Wilson and Tumulty protected the President from needless interruptions and wasteful interviews, but even so the number of persons he had to see was enormous. Few were as considerate as George Creel, who understood his chief's "sense of urgency" and prepared his business ahead of time with care and precision. After a full day, Wilson generally devoted his evenings to the preparation of important papers and confidential correspondence, pecking away at his typewriter in the quiet of his study, while his wife read or answered letters near by. Often it was after midnight before he snapped out his old, green-shaded lamp and went to bed.

He was nearly always tired. "I could go to sleep at an angle of ninety-five degrees," he once told Creel. Sleep was for him completely relaxing. Mrs. Wilson reports that it was the sleep of the dead: utterly motionless. Sometimes it was frightening—he seemed not even to breathe—and she would bend over him to make sure he was really alive. He would awaken completely refreshed. When sleep was impossible he could find relaxation even from gazing for a few moments at some distant object; between interviews, for instance, he would go to the window and fix his eyes on a bush on the White House grounds. When his next visitor was ushered in, he would face him with renewed vitality. He also found relief at lunch and dinner. He tried to keep his meals free from politics, reserving them for his family, though Secretary McAdoo, being his son-in-law, sometimes broke this "rule" when he was present.

Whenever the press of work became too great, Mrs. Wilson would intervene, forcing him to go for a drive, attend the theater, or play a round of golf. ("He doesn't play . . . a long game, but his direction is simply re-markable," one golfing companion has recorded. "He is invariably straight down the course.") In such ways he managed to bear his heavy burdens, though more and more, visitors noticed how gaunt he was becoming.

Amid the hectic, fatiguing struggle to mobilize the nation and win the war, Wilson still found time to plan for the peace that was to come. His hopes were high, his motives pure. Victory, he saw, would only clear the way to make the world safe for democracy and justify the cruel war. The making of peace was to be, he fondly hoped, the culminating glory of his life.

VIII

ON June 14, 1917 Woodrow Wilson stood before the Washington Monument in a driving rain to make a speech. His immediate audience, huddled beneath sodden umbrellas, had gathered to commemorate Flag Day, and the President spoke eloquently of "the emblem of our unity, our power, our thought and purpose." But the simple ceremony on the green between the Capitol and the White House expressed something more than patriotism.

The first great Liberty Loan drive was drawing to a close, producing in profusion the dollars that were to make victory possible. The vast American war machine was slowly beginning to roll, while the perilous road ahead called for still greater efforts.

At the same time there were compelling reasons for promoting a just peace. The Czar of Russia had recently been overthrown, and his liberal successors, struggling to maintain themselves against the threats of communist and reactionary extremists, were demanding the promise of a peace "without annexations or indemnities" as the price of continued participation in the brutal struggle. Liberals in other Allied nations, grown pessimistic in the face of continued bloodshed and repressed liberties, needed encouragement. Further, German morale might well be sapped by an appeal for a humane settlement.

To fight ruthlessly but with altruistic aims: this was Wilson's self-imposed task. To accomplish it, he was bound to stir his people's passions to a point where they would kill without mercy, but he had also to persuade them that, once victorious, they must bind up their en-

emy's wounds along with their own, and view dispassionately the terms of peace. He was driven to this position by
conscience, ego, and the need to justify his past actions.
He attacked the problem with all his energy and eloquence.

He had outlined his strategy in his April address to
Congress. On Flag Day he elaborated on it. Germany
was the enemy—evil, crafty, ambitious, and callous. Her
armies stood astride the heart of Europe, her "agents and
dupes" worked nefariously all over the globe, even in
America. Should she triumph, Europe would be lost to
barbarism and autocracy, the United States would become a nation of bayonets, and soon the world would
again be convulsed by war. But the foe was *Germany*,
not the Germans. Not the people—"they are not our
enemies." Allied victory must surely weaken "the military masters under whom Germany is bleeding," and
then "their people will thrust them aside." Thus "the
People's War" would bring freedom and justice to everyone, "the German peoples themselves included."

Wilson was attempting an act of statesmanship of the
most difficult and complex type. He was trying to devise
a single policy that would both win the war and assure a
fair settlement when the war was over, and this required
the most delicate balancing of contradictory forces. There
was, for example, the danger that by stressing the guilt-
lessness of the German people, the Allies' will to fight
might be weakened. Yet how else prepare the world for
a peace without revenge, conquest, and selfish aggrandizement? Again, Wilson promised that from the ugliness
of war there would rise a splendid new world. He was
convinced that this was possible; his faith would not let
him think otherwise. But was it possible? He gave all
his strength to prove that it was, and certainly he accom-

plished a very great deal. He can hardly be condemned if he did not entirely succeed. But perhaps he should have sought for less. In the end he might have found more.

Wilson's view of the war was somewhat distorted. There was no factual evidence behind his claim that the Kaiser's government did not represent the will of most German citizens. There is grave doubt too that the American people accepted this distinction—at least not as completely as Wilson liked to assume. Wilson also failed to understand all the implications of his theory of the war. His hopes were predicated on the idea that the Allies were as ready as America for a just peace. Yet he knew from three years of neutrality that this was not so. He was careful to insist that the other nations fighting Germany were our "associates," not our "allies." He pre-served the independent organization of the American army when it finally reached France, and in countless minor ways remained aloof, although he maintained in public speeches the unshakable unity and high purpose of all concerned.

In general, when conflicts developed between his plans for winning the war and his plans for making the world safe for democracy, the former took precedence. This was natural enough, even essential, in that victory was basic to all his fond hopes. But Wilson often would not face frankly the problems he was creating for him-self. During his period of desperate soul-searching before America entered the conflict, he told a friendly newspa-perman: "Once lead this people into war, and they'll forget there ever was such a thing as tolerance. . . . The spirit of ruthless brutality will enter into the very fiber of our national life, infecting Congress, the courts, the policeman on the beat, the man in the street." But before the war was over he put his signature to a bill that made it illegal to criticize the United States Government, the flag, or even the uniform of an American sailor (with its absurd, thirteen-button fly). This was done to check sedition and espionage, but one of the law's by-products was a frenzied witch-hunt during which Fritz Kreisler was prevented from playing his violin in public, sauerkraut was renamed "liberty cabbage," German books (and even the language itself) were banned in schools, and dozens of harmless individuals were thrown into prison. Hatred of "the Hun" coursed through the populace, while the President composed lofty speeches about tolerance and "peace without victory." This policy may have helped win the war, but it was poor preparation for a just peace.

There is much evidence that Wilson was dismayed by the passions that swept America in 1917 and 1918, though they might have been less violent had he been more alert in defending civil liberties. But, sometimes without realizing it, he sacrificed the bright future of his dreams in other ways. Early in January 1918 he laid down his blueprint for the world settlement—the famous Fourteen Points.

This statement of long-range objectives was occasioned by short-range needs. The Bolsheviks had seized control in Russia and were peppering the world with condemnations of the war as a selfish, imperialistic struggle for power. If their arguments went unanswered, Wilson told the British Ambassador, "the effect would be great and would increase." Something had to be done to check Communism, to fortify the Allied peoples, and to undermine the German will to resist. Wilson summoned Colonel House to Washington. He arrived on Friday evening, January 4. "Saturday was a remarkable day,"

House wrote later in his diary. "We actually got down to work at half-past ten and finished remaking the map of the world, as we would have it, at half-past twelve o'clock."

The Fourteen Points, as presented in an address to Congress on January 8, were thus primarily propaganda, although they also reflected Wilson's sincere desires. "The day of conquest and aggrandizement is gone by," the President orated. "What we demand in this war . . . is that the world be made fit and safe to live in." First of all, the peace conference must be conducted in the full view of the world, not in secret. "Open covenants of peace, openly arrived at." It must provide for complete freedom of the seas "alike in peace and in war," must break down the barriers to international trade, reduce armaments, reorganize the control of all colonial areas in the interests of native peoples, and redraw the boundaries of Europe in accord with the principle of national self-determination. This last was elaborated in a bill of particulars: Captured Russian territory was to be restored, Belgium evacuated, and Alsace-Lorraine returned to France. Austria-Hungary's heterogeneous nationalities were to be granted a measure of autonomy, Italian frontiers were to be readjusted "along clearly recognizable lines of nationality," the Balkans made free, Turkey divested of her subject peoples. An "independent Polish state," buttressed by "a free and secure access to the sea," should be set up and maintained by international agreement. Finally (and in Wilson's mind most important of all), "a general association of nations must be formed under specific covenants for the purpose of affording mutual guarantees of political independence and territorial integrity to great and small states alike."

The immediate impact of the speech was not impres-

sive. American reactions were almost uniformly good;
the Allies also approved, although with some reservations
about specific points. The British, for example, expressed suspicion of "freedom of the seas," and the Italians were not charmed by the implication that their
claims to non-Italian territory in the northern Adriatic
region would be disregarded. But the speech did not
cause an outbreak of unrest among enemy liberals as
Wilson had hoped, and the Russians viewed it suspi-
ciously, interpreting it (correctly enough) as a capitalist
plot to keep them in a war they were determined to abandon at all costs. Isolated cynics pointed out the difficulties that would beset any reconstruction of national
boundaries on ethnic lines in heterogeneous central Europe. How was Poland, for instance, to obtain access to
the sea unless large, predominantly German areas were
turned over to her?

But the points that one group disliked, others approved, and few dared quarrel with Wilson's purpose.
Nobody could complain about general points, like disarmament, although no one was any more specific than
Wilson in explaining how disarmament was to be accomplished.

The effect of the speech was not what Wilson had expected. The Fourteen Points were designed for two purposes. The short-range objective was propagandistic—to
strengthen Allied morale and weaken German. The
long-range objective was to lay the foundations for an
altruistic settlement of the war. But in fact, the immediate
result was the stimulation of interest in a just peace without materially affecting anyone's will to fight. The
Bolsheviks were unmoved; shortly thereafter they surrendered abjectly to the Central Powers, enabling the Germans to throw the main weight of their armies against

the Western front. The Germans considered the Fourteen Points "a masterpiece of effrontery." Their will to
fight was not weakened. On the other hand, the hopes of
well-meaning people all over the world for a just and
humane peace came into focus as soon as they read Wilson's speech.

In the long run, however, the results were quite the
reverse. In the spring of 1918 the Germans' power was
at its height. By the summer their last great drive in
France had been smashed, and the Allies were beginning to push them back to final defeat. As their cause
became more and more hopeless, the *propaganda* effect of
the Fourteen Points increased in force. Faced with destruction, the German populace was soon ready to cease
fighting and accept peace without victory. Wilson's
speech did much to shorten the war.

But at this juncture the unrealistic aspects of the
Points became a handicap in achieving the long-range objective. Statesmen who had been untroubled by their
vagueness and contradictions when victory was still a
distant dream suddenly began to consider them in detail,
and weigh them against the selfish advantages they hoped
to gain. Fine-sounding slogans like "self-determination"
and "freedom of the seas" led inevitably to misunderstanding, distortion, and frustration. Hopes raised heav-
enward by well-meaning idealism then crashed to sinful
earth. Wilson conceded too much to the need for winning the war in January 1918. Less ambitious peace aims
would have been just as effective, and would have been
far easier to carry out when the day of settlement finally
dawned.

The autumn of 1918 found Wilson at the pinnacle of
his career. By October the military might of the Central

Powers was crumbling on every side as the weight of American power finally tipped the balance and ended the long stalemate. When the German armies fell back and an invasion of the Fatherland loomed, the Kaiser's ministers changed their view of the Fourteen Points, and sounded out the President about peace negotiations. Wilson deftly exploited the situation. He informed them that peace on the basis of the Fourteen Points was available to the "veritable representatives of the German people," but to "the military masters of the monarchical autocrats of Germany" he could offer no terms but unconditional surrender.

This was like dangling a carrot before the nose of a donkey. Without actually demanding that the people revolt against their leaders (which might have caused a reaction in favor of the German bitter-enders), Wilson undermined their will to fight on by implying that less harsh terms would be offered to a new liberal government. His statement stirred up internal dissension in Germany at a time when the military situation was already desperate and the only hope lay in single-minded devotion to the cause. It unquestionably hastened the revolution that swept the Kaiser from his throne, shortening the war and saving countless lives. Thus, without sacrificing his plans for a fair peace, Wilson contributed greatly to the demoralization and defeat of the enemy.

At the same time he confounded his American critics like Theodore Roosevelt and Lodge, for he forced the Germans to accept an armistice that left them helpless. "There is no object in trying to be smart in diplomatic notes with Germany," Lodge complained to a friend. "The thing to do is to lick Germany and tell her what arrangements we are going to make." But Lodge had to concede that Wilson had been "smart"—for him a very great concession indeed. When Germany accepted Wilson's "ultimatum" and internal chaos in the Empire made protracted resistance impossible, Wilson coolly turned the whole problem of negotiating an armistice over to the Allied Supreme War Council, which, in turn, pressed its own terms on the prostrate foe. Wilson's handling of the diplomatic exchanges had been brilliant.

Having exploited thoroughly the appeal of the Fourteen Points to the enemy, Wilson felt morally obligated to insist that the Allies also accept them as the basis for peace. Otherwise America might justly be accused of double-dealing. Therefore, in late October, the President sent Colonel House to Paris to consult with Allied leaders. House saw at once that the Allies would be difficult to deal with. As victory became daily more certain, their interest in the spoils of war increased correspondingly. "If we do not use care," House noted only two days after arriving, "we shall place ourselves in some such dishonorable position as Germany when she violated her treaty obligations as to Belgium."

But it would be unfair to explain the Allies' viewpoint only in terms of selfishness. They had all suffered tremendous losses. Hatred of the enemy was naturally very strong. They were also aware (more aware than Wilson) of the great difficulties involved in writing a peace treaty. And they were troubled by the vagueness of the Fourteen Points. Just what was "freedom of the seas"? What did "open covenants of peace openly arrived at" mean?

House tried to correct the vagueness by having a commentary on the Points prepared which became the "official" American interpretation. Its general effect was to narrow Wilson's program and make it less drastic. When Premier Clemenceau of France read the original point condemning secret diplomacy, he stated flatly: "I cannot agree never to make a private or secret diplomatic agreement of any kind." The British representative, Lloyd George, backed him fully. "I do not think it possible so to limit oneself," he told House. But the commentary explained that "the phrase was not meant to exclude confidential diplomatic negotiations"; its purpose was only to insure that the *results* of the negotiations would be published to the world. In effect, of course, this meant that "openly arrived at" had absolutely no significance. So defined, the Allied leaders found the point unexceptionable.

In their watered-down form, most of the Points seemed at worst harmless to the European diplomats, but even so, House experienced grave difficulties in getting then accepted. The greatest snag was Point Two, concerning freedom of the seas in wartime. On its face it seemed to involve abandoning the right of blockade, and this England would not consider. House's commentary weakened the point a good deal, but Lloyd George considered the right of blockade so vital that he still refused to agree, and the others, dissatisfied with the Points for their own reasons, supported him. House then made "the longest speech of his life":

If the Allies are unwilling to accept the Fourteen Points . . . there can be, as far as I can see, only one course for the President to pursue. He would have to tell the Germans that the conditions which they had accepted are not acceptable to the powers with which America *has been* associated. America would then have to take up direct negotiations with Germany and Austria.

The implications were at once obvious to all. Lloyd George bounced to his feet. "Would that mean a separate peace between America and the Central Powers?"

he asked. "It might well," House replied gravely. ("My statement," he later telegraphed Wilson with typical restraint, "had a very exciting effect on those present.") Everyone became conciliatory. If America withdrew from the war victory might slip away.

But Lloyd George was preeminently a practical man. "If the United States made a separate peace," he said plaintively but with determination, "we would be sorry, but we could not give up the blockade." "Yes," chimed in Clemenceau. "War would not be war if there was freedom of the seas."

Finally House settled for a statement by the British that they would "discuss" freedom of the seas at the peace conference, and all agreed that the Fourteen Points should be the basis for the negotiations. House considered this a great diplomatic triumph; Wilson a matter-of-fact acceptance of undebatable principles. The British viewed the agreement as a well-intentioned compromise, the Italians as a surrender of the chief purposes of the war, and the French as a meaningless mouthing of impossible ideals. "God gave us the Ten Commandments, and we broke them," the cynical Clemenceau is said to have remarked. "Wilson gives us the Fourteen Points. We shall see."

There was some substance to all these views, and also to the position taken later by the Germans, who cried duplicity, arguing that they had agreed to one set of points and the Allies to another. It is true that the Allies were reluctant converts to a peace with justice, and that Wilson surrendered much of the idealism of his Points without a fight and perhaps without realizing what he was doing. He might, as a disillusioned liberal was later to say, have "reduced the Allied leaders to pulp" by really threatening a separate peace and by cutting off American loans, more desperately needed after the armistice than before.

But taken all in all, House had represented the interests of his chief admirably. Given the error already made in espousing a program so vague and unrealistic, House salvaged more than could reasonably have been expected from the midst of the passions of the last days of war. When the armistice was formalized on November 11, all the great nations were in signed agreement that they would fashion a fair and unselfish treaty. Men of good will the world over sensed this, and in the first ecstatic days after the guns fell silent, they revered Woodrow Wilson as few living men have ever been revered.

Yet the very masses who praised Wilson's high-mindedness were full of unreasoning hatred of the foe. Those who were heartened by the President's vision of a league of nations still cheered far more lustily for their own several flags. As millions laid down their arms and joined in celebration and prayer, such contradictions were forgotten, but only for the moment.

Wilson was aware of the difficulties ahead. He suspected the motives of the Allied leaders, who, he thought, did not represent the will of their own peoples. So he made the unprecedented decision to go to Paris himself, and to take part in the deliberations of the peace conference in order to insure the triumph of his plans.

In going he committed a grave error of judgment. At the time he was criticized for violating the "tradition" that a President should not leave the country while in office. But his real error was in misunderstanding the nature of his task. Wilson had to fight a battle on two fronts, one in Europe where the peace treaty was to be fabricated, the other in America where the finished product had to face the challenge of isolationism and partisanship. He

assumed that the European battle would be more difficult to win, because, in the last analysis, he did not think
the leaders of the Allies wanted a fair and humane peace.
Their people did, he felt, but not the politicians themselves.

This view was mistaken to begin with, for the Allied
statesmen, taken together, were honest and well-intentioned, if somewhat lacking in vision. The masses, the
same masses that were to cheer Wilson to the skies, were
actually the chief obstacle to his program. The people of
England, for example, were solely responsible for Lloyd
George's stubborn refusal to consider freedom of the
seas. "I could not accept the principle of the Freedom of
the Seas," the stocky Prime Minister had confessed to
House. "It's no good saying I accept the principle. It
would only mean that in a week's time a new Prime
Minister would be here who would say that he could not
accept this principle. The English people will not look
at it." Wilson would have done well to trust the Allied
statesmen a little more; he should have let others represent the United States at the peace table, preserving his
aloofness, and exercising his great influence at a distance.

On the other hand, in November 1918, Wilson already had ample evidence that his presence in America
would be urgently needed. He had tried to make the
1918 congressional elections a test of his leadership, and
failed ignominiously. His "Appeal" to the people for a
Democratic Congress had been disregarded; the Republicans captured control of both Houses. As far as the
United States was concerned, what good would *any* labor in Paris accomplish if the Senate failed to ratify the
resultant treaty? The Republicans had interpreted his
"Appeal" as rank and unjust partisanship. They were
ready to retort in kind. Against such odds, Wilson's job

was to persuade his people to abandon their isolationist prejudices and join a league of nations. A great educational campaign was clearly in order, as well as all the high-powered politicking the Chief Executive could muster. In addition, countless domestic problems of demobilization and reconversion to a peacetime economy were certain to arise. Wilson faced two great challenges to his leadership, but the domestic one more urgently required direct, personal management, and the particular qualities he possessed in abundance.

But nothing could stop him; he was determined to go. Nearly all his advisers were against his going. Colonel House, already on the scene in Paris, tried as hard as he ever did to change the presidential mind. "Americans here whose opinions are of any value are practically unanimous . . . that it would be unwise for you to sit in the Peace Conference," he cabled. Wilson replied with unusual sharpness: "Your telegram upsets every plan we have made. . . . I infer that the French and British leaders desire to exclude me . . . for fear that I might lead the weaker nations against them. . . . It is universally expected and generally desired here [!] that I should attend the Conference." Such peremptory language was usually enough to silence House at once, but so strongly did he feel that he cabled again: "My judgment is that you should determine on your arrival here what share it is wise for you to take in the proceedings." He tried to persuade Wilson to attend only the preliminary sessions, and return to America when the real work began. But he had no influence.

Most of those who advised against his going did so for the wrong reason. They were no better than Wilson at appraising the importance of domestic politics. They felt, as Secretary of State Lansing wrote, that as a delegate the President would lose his "unique position" above the battle and become "a prey to intrigue" and crafty diplomacy.

Political opponents accused Wilson of egotism, of wanting to become "President of the World." This was unfair. He would not have been human if the thought of participating had not been pleasant, but he saw it clearly as a matter of duty. He spoke with full candor to Fuel Administrator Harry Garfield, an old friend of his Princeton days, who had joined in the chorus against his attending the conference. "There is much in what you say, Harry," he admitted soberly. "I am indeed confronted with a difficult decision. But now listen to me and weigh my thought. Here in America I understand what is going on. . . . But Europe is far away, and the voices that come to me from there are so confusing."

He *must* go! "I believe in a Divine Providence," he told his secretary. "It is my belief that no body of men however they concert their power or their influence can defeat this great world enterprise." Nor, he might have added, could any man refuse the call to battle for the divine cause.

Wilson selected four men to accompany him as commissioners. Secretary of State Lansing was an obvious choice, but the other three were most unconventional appointments. Colonel House, while well-qualified by his wartime services, had never held an important public office. General Tasker H. Bliss, the third member, was intelligent, hard-working, and efficient, but without political stature or diplomatic experience. On the other hand, Henry White, who completed the group, was a career diplomat. Yet he was picked because he was a Republican, and as a sop to the G.O.P. he was pitifully inadequate.

The choice of commissioners again demonstrated Wilson's failure to appreciate the importance of domestic politics. The ratification of the peace treaty by a Senate controlled by Republicans was sure to be his biggest problem. He should have included at least one powerful Republican, preferably a senator, and probably a leading Democratic senator too. Bliss, House, and White need not have been sacrificed; all could have gone along in the army of "experts" who made up the full delegation, and done their jobs just as effectively.

Wilson did give some thought to including an important member of the opposition. One by one he ticked off prominent Republican statesmen: this one because he was on record for a harsh peace, another because he had criticized the administration during the war, someone else for reasons of personal antipathy. He could rationalize a case against each, but the fact that the entire roster was discarded shows that his own peculiar personality lay at the heart of his difficulty. He wanted harmony in the delegation, but on his own terms; he wanted intelligent advisers but not self-willed ones. Men like Ex-President Taft and Former Senator Elihu Root—the most frequently mentioned Republican candidates—might carry discussion beyond the offering of advice into the realm of argument, and Wilson had no stomach for argument. It was too personal, too individual, too emotional. Professor Bailey has put it well: Wilson, he wrote, "could not bring himself" to pick the likes of Taft or Root. "The tragedy is that he was temperamentally incapable either of inviting them or of serving wholeheartedly with them." The result, as the cynical Lodge sneered, was that he appointed himself four times—and Henry White.

There was criticism, but great events were in the making and the harmful effects of his selections would not be felt for months. Whatever his failings, Wilson had come to grips with a noble ideal, and the hopes of humanity rode with him on the *George Washington* as he sailed for Paris. "Tell me what's right and I'll fight for it," he begged the formidable collection of experts he was taking with him, and the patent sincerity of his plea touched millions of hearts. Candles burned before his picture in simple homes the world over. Streets were named in his honor by enthusiastic communities. As he boarded the liner a sweatshop worker commented reverently: "There goes the man who is going to change all this for us."

Seeds of future troubles lay in this homage, but Wilson drew much-needed strength from it as well. For he was tired. The strains of war had levied a heavy toll on a man never strong and now past sixty. On the boat, steaming slowly eastward through December seas, he slept for hours, woke, and slept again.

The ship reached Brest at last, gliding into the harbor through a lane of Allied warships thundering their presidential salutes. The dawn had been shrouded in mists, but as the *George Washington*'s anchor rumbled into the sea, the sun burst forth. It was Friday the thirteenth, a date ominous in sailors' eyes, but encouraging to Wilson, who always maintained that thirteen was his lucky number. Rested and ready, smiling and waving his high silk hat, he descended to the tender, *Gun,* and bobbed across the choppy harbor toward the cheering city.

IX

WHEN Wilson stepped ashore at Brest half a continent went mad with joy. The streets of the port were lined with welcomers—soldiers, school children, peasants from the country districts in bright-colored Breton costumes. The city fathers met him at the wharf and bore him through the town under triumphal arches. *"Vive l'Amérique! Vive le Président! Vive Vil-s-o-n!"*

There were speeches of welcome, and President Poincaré sent his private train to carry the hero to Paris. As the special roared eastward through the Côtes du Nord in the early winter twilight, farmers gathered along the tracks to cheer him on his way. Every station was crowded with well-wishers, and long after darkness had fallen, the passengers' sleep was interrupted from time to time by muffled ovations as peasants and townspeople came together in the night to cheer and pray.

At Paris the welcome was almost beyond description. The chains were withdrawn before the Arc de Triomphe, and Wilson and President Poincaré rode beneath it in a carriage at the head of a great parade. The procession moved down the broad Champs Élysées, the boulevard lined solidly to the Place de la Concorde with French troops, restraining a crowd of two millions. Flowers rained down upon the President and his party; the cheers were deafening and unceasing. Mrs. Wilson grew giddy trying to respond to the endless ovation as the parade moved on through the heart of the city to the palace of Prince Murat, where she and her husband were to reside.

Other men have received great ovations, but few so sustained. For Wilson's did not end when the doors of Prince Murat's magnificent mansion closed behind him.

He was ready to go to work at once, but there were vex-
ing delays. The complexities of this mammoth conference made for a vast inertia. There were ceremonies, introductions, "arrangements," and state visits to be taken
care of. The Christmas season was about to begin, and
bewildered diplomats welcomed additional time to ap-
praise the chaotic German situation, for the outcome of
the revolution there was still unclear. The President, with
time on his hands, consented to visit England and Italy,
where he was again feted by the multitudes.

In England the public was comparatively restrained,
although, as one correspondent noted: "The profound
respect and regard with which the men removed their
hats and the women bowed and waved were beyond
mistaking." But the official reception was impressive even
by British standards. The King and Queen treated the
Wilsons as cherished friends; the President addressed
the people from a Buckingham Palace balcony; he un-
veiled a portrait of George Washington at Number Ten
Downing Street.

His reception in Italy was staggering. "Voovro Veel-
son" was hailed as the "god of peace," and wounded soldiers tried to kiss his clothes. When he failed to make a
scheduled appearance in the Piazza Venezia in Rome,
women wept and men tossed away their hats and tore
their hair.

No man could remain unaffected by such acclaim.
Wilson, given his particular nature and his preconceived
ideas about the desires of the peoples of western Europe,
was deeply moved, and more important, reassured in his
determination to fight for a just peace. He was more than
ever convinced that the statesmen in Paris did not truly
represent their own people and that *he* must represent
these people if their voices were to be heard at all.

How wrong he was! The same day that he reached Paris the British electorate gave Lloyd George a resounding vote of confidence on his promise to squeeze Germany "until the pips squeak." While the President was responding to the cheers of Great Britain, Clemenceau obtained the largest majority of his career in the Chamber of Deputies by defending the old balance of power. To Wilson these events proved that the politicians were wicked men. A simpler explanation would have been closer to the truth. Perhaps the politicians did not resist the popular desire for revenge and the spoils of war, but the desire was there. Sometime later Wilson asked Lloyd George, whom he liked instinctively, why he had promised the voters to hang the Kaiser and exact harsh terms from Germany, and why he had called an election so soon after the armistice. "It is well for me that the election came as early as it did," the Prime Minister replied ruefully. "Otherwise I might have had to promise more."

The wheels of the peace conference finally began to turn about the middle of January. Even then they moved with irritating slowness, for dozens of delegations, made up of thousands of individuals, had to be co-ordinated. Strange to relate, there was no agenda, no over-all plan other than a few brief principal topics laid down by Wilson. "I feel as if we . . . were like a lot of skilled workmen who are ordered to build a house," Secretary Lansing wrote on January 16. "We have the materials and tools, but there are no plans and specifications and no master-workman in charge of the construction. We putter around in an aimless sort of way and get nowhere."

Progress was further hampered by the whole atmosphere surrounding the conference. Paris had been under virtual siege for four years. Crippled veterans stumped the streets; black arm-bands and other signs of mourning

were common sights. "Everyone was afraid of being
called a pro-German," one witness recorded. "We felt
like surgeons operating in the ballroom with the aunts of
the patient gathered all around." At the same time the
traditional gaiety of the city was a further distraction.
Hotels were jammed, chic restaurants crowded at all
hours, tickets to the opera and the theater almost unob-
tainable. Official receptions, teas, and dinner parties com-
peted with informal social affairs for the time of the great
dignitaries. The government-inspired press added to the
tension with unrestrained attacks on delay and any sign
of softness toward the defeated foe.[1]

Yet the confusion, the emotionalism, and the distractions surrounding the Versailles Conference can be over-
emphasized. Everyone, as Ray Stannard Baker noted,
"was struck with a kind of historic awe." The world was
being refashioned, the future determined. Most of the

---

[1] Harold Nicolson has given us this vivid picture of the city
in the early months of 1919: *Were I to sketch . . . a scenario of
my own impressions, the result would be something as follows.
As a recurrent undertone throughout would run the rumble of
Time's winged chariot: incessantly reiterant would come the
motif of this time-pressure—newspapers screaming in headlines
against the Dawdlers of Paris, the clamour for demobilization,
"Get the Boys back," the starving millions of Central Europe,
the slouching queues of prisoners still behind their barbed wire,
the flames of communism flaring. . . . Through this . . . would
pierce the sharper discordances of other sounds: the machine-
gun rattle of a million typewriters, the incessant shrilling of tel-
ephones, the clatter of motor bicycles, the drone of aeroplanes,
the cold voices of interpreters, "le délégé des Etats-Unis con-
state qu'il ne peut se ranger . . ." the blare of trumpets, the
thunder of guns saluting at the Invalides, the rustling of files, a
woman in a black woollen shawl singing "Madelon" in front of
a café, a crackle of Rolls Royces upon the gravel of sumptuous
courtyards, and throughout the sound of footsteps hurrying now
upon the parquet of some gallery, now upon the stone stairway
of some Ministry, and now muffled on the heavy Aubusson of
some overheated saloon.*

major participants, and dozens of lesser figures, kept diaries or other records of their doings and impressions, determined to preserve for posterity every possible recollection of the great conference. They worked hard, and for long hours, and they accomplished much. None drove himself more mercilessly than Wilson.

Control of the conference passed quickly into the hands of the Council of Ten (made up of two delegates from each of the five great powers, the United States, France, Great Britain, Italy, and Japan). As representatives of the three most powerful nations, Wilson, Lloyd George, and Clemenceau were the dominant figures. Along with Orlando of Italy they eventually (as the Big Four) came to make most of the crucial decisions themselves. Despite his distrust of these statesmen, Wilson was courtesy itself in his dealings with them. No matter how bitter the opposition or long-drawn-out the debate, he never displayed anger or impatience. Clemenceau frequently dozed when some matter of no importance to France was under discussion, and Lloyd George was often guilty of amazing ignorance about important points, but Wilson listened carefully to each word, and crammed for hours in an effort to master every complicated aspect of the settlement. When he spoke himself, he leaned forward intently across the table holding tight to the arms of his chair as if to maintain his balance, addressing first one and then another of the delegates in earnest yet quiet tones, and always with perfect diction and polished phrases.

As spokesman for the host nation, Georges Clemenceau presided at the Council of Ten. He was then eighty years old, stooped, white-haired, with wrinkled face and sallow complexion, but his powerful jaw, jutting out below his gray walrus mustache, indicated determination

and forcefulness. He was called "the Tiger," and with
good reason, for he was a fighter. During the war he
played a role not unlike Winston Churchill's in World
War II, rallying his people in their darkest hour and
leading them on through grueling trials to final triumph.
He was a realist and a cynic, and he hated all things
German. At a meeting of the Supreme War Council
shortly before the armistice he said, only half humor-
ously: "The only thing we aren't taking from Germany
are the Kaiser's pants." He viewed Wilson with amused
contempt, nicknaming him "Jupiter." "I can get on with
you," he once told House. "I understand you. But talking to Wilson is something like talking to Jesus Christ!"
For his part, the President believed that Clemenceau had
a "feminine" mind. Like the girls at Bryn Mawr, he was
good at dealing with specific problems but weak in handling generalities. "He is like an old dog trying to find a
place to rest," Wilson told Ray Stannard Baker. "He
turns slowly around following his tail, before he gets
down to it."

Wilson's relations with Lloyd George were at once
friendlier and more complicated. Like Clemenceau, the
Britain was short, thick-set and full of animal vitality,
but he had a baby-pink face and a thick shock of white
hair. He possessed ability and intelligence, but was essentially a man of feeling rather than of thought. As was
said by a member of the British delegation, Lloyd George
had an "unerring, almost medium-like, sensibility to everyone immediately around him." Few could resist his
charm, and since, more often than not, he sided with the
President against Clemenceau's determination to crush
Germany, Wilson liked him, and came frequently to rely
upon him for support. But his bouncy informality, slap-
dash approach to the details of the treaty, and, above all,

his utter disregard of consistency and principle were alien
to Wilson's serious intensity of purpose. "If you want to
succeed in politics, you must keep your conscience well
under control," Lloyd George once told an English
statesman. This, of course, would have horrified Wilson.

Although the two were in intimate contact for months,
their points of view were so at odds that they never really
understood each other. Lloyd George was puzzled by
Wilson's sermonettes on "right being more important
than might, and justice being more eternal than force."
Did the President, he wondered, actually believe these
things? "He was the most extraordinary compound I
have ever encountered," the Prime Minister wrote in his
memoirs. Wilson could never fathom the Prime Minister's monumental shifts of position, nor his casual ability
to override logic. Once, when they were engaged in a
tense discussion of the knotty Italian frontier question,
Lloyd George suddenly interjected Australia into the
conversation. "[Prime Minister] Hughes is very bitter,
Mr. President," he said solicitously. "He says that great
America suffered fewer casualties in the war than little
Australia, yet you oppose all her just claims."

Wilson failed to follow the trend of the talk, but he
was quick to defend himself. "Do you mean to minimize
our contribution or to deny that through our assistance
the war was brought to a successful conclusion? "

"Of course not, of course not," Lloyd George assured
him. Then, with magnificent disregard of logic, he
added: "However, we are so far apart as to many problems, let us not pursue this prickly question further." The
thread of the conversation was completely lost—Italy,
Australia, America—what *were* they discussing? Yet the
tension was gone with it. Clemenceau, the realist,
brought them back to business. "I made war, now I want

to make peace," he commented sarcastically. "I hope you will help me."

Wilson's difficulties with Clemenceau and Lloyd George were inevitable. In the main, he made the best of them, and contrary to the opinions of many critics, he was seldom "bamboozled" by wily European diplomats at Paris. Usually his knowledge of the specific problems discussed was greater than theirs. He had brought with him an imposing group of experts on European affairs. Harold Nicolson, himself a British "expert," has written: "I have never had to work with a body of men more intelligent, more scholarly, more broad-minded or more accurately informed than were the American Delegation to the Peace Conference. On every occasion where I differed from their opinion I have since realized that I was wrong and they were right."

Wilson made excellent use of these highly qualified specialists. Since they stood in positions clearly subordinate to him, he was able to take their advice freely. "I never saw a man more ready and anxious to consult than he," one financial expert recalled. "I never saw a man more considerate of . . . his coadjutors . . . nor a man more ready to give them credit with the other chiefs of state." Indeed, Wilson was, if anything, too concerned with the technical aspects of the treaty. He maintained a private wire connecting him with Delegation Headquarters at the Crillon, and was constantly calling for documents, maps, and expert opinions. Douglas W. Johnson, an expert on boundaries, recorded that on one occasion Wilson even roused him from his bed in the middle of the night inquiring after some papers that had not arrived as promised. Mrs. Wilson once found the President on his hands and knees with a group of specialists puzzling over some maps. "You look like a lot of little boys playing a game," she said. "Alas," he replied, "it is the most serious game ever undertaken."

In the attempt to master every aspect of all the questions before the conference Wilson taxed his limited strength and left himself with less energy than he needed for his crucial discussions with the other leaders. And sometimes his tired brain was so cluttered with unrelated scraps of information that he was incapable of seeing the whole picture in perspective.

Considering his dependence upon the experts, it is strange, yet entirely consistent with his personality, that the President made almost no use of his fellow American commissioners. Except for Colonel House, he practically ignored them, and gave them little or nothing to do. Secretary Lansing, who should have been his right hand, was repeatedly snubbed. Lansing's letters and suggestions were disregarded. When Wilson was absent from the conference, House, not the Secretary of State, sat in his place. Wilson never had a high opinion of Lansing, having appointed him when Bryan resigned only because it was easier to promote him than to cast about in the emergency for a new person. "All I want is a good clerk, and he's a good clerk," the President said contemptuously at that time. Lansing was not brilliant. He was conservative, reserved, and unimaginatively realistic. But he had ability, and was a good diplomat. Henry White, a man of tremendous experience in international affairs, thought highly of his performance at Paris.

Wilson's dislike seems to have been purely personal. Lansing was an inveterate and ambidextrous "doodler." Like all good "doodlers" he could practice his intricate art during a conference without losing for a moment the thread of the discussion, but the habit annoyed his chief.

More important, Lansing did not know when to stop arguing with Wilson. He was a lawyer (another strike
against him in Wilson's book), and thus perhaps more
contentious than was necessary. "I persevered in my efforts to induce him to abandon in some cases or to modify
in others a course which would in my judgment be a violation of principle or a mistake in policy," Lansing confessed in his memoirs. With Wilson, this was fatal. Only
the fear that Lansing's dismissal would disrupt the conference, and his own dislike of open quarrels, kept Wilson from demanding the Secretary's resignation. While
he did not actively dislike the other commissioners, he
made little effort to discover their views or utilize their
talents, thus losing a great deal of the help they could
have given him.

But with or without assistance, Wilson labored zealously over the treaty. And though he dealt with all its
aspects, one element was always central in his mind—
the creation of a league of nations. He had first given serious thought to the idea of a post-war international organization in 1916, when he made his great effort to end
the war by diplomacy. It became more important to him
as a result of his personal struggle to justify American
participation in the conflict, for it was apparent that the
better world he envisioned would need an international
policeman of some kind. The league was the last and
most important of his Fourteen Points of January 1918.
He had delegated to Colonel House the responsibility for
drawing up a specific plan, and in August 1918 the two
men conferred in Massachusetts, revising and editing
House's draft. These plans were kept secret, for Wilson
believed that premature publication would only provoke
controversy.

At Paris, House and other American experts con

sulted with the British, who had also been working on a
draft for a league. The two groups were never far apart,
and after some negotiation, Wilson agreed to accept the
British scheme as the basis for forging what he liked to
call "the Covenant." On January 25 a plenary session of
the Versailles Conference unanimously approved the
league principle, and set up a committee to prepare a
charter, providing that the organization should be made
an integral part of the peace treaty. Wilson had insisted
upon integration from the start, and made his point over
heavy opposition.

The main argument against including the League in
the treaty was the pressing need for speed. Central Europe was close to chaos; communism was spreading rapidly; people were literally starving to death. While a
technical state of war continued, nothing could be done
about demobilizing the troops, or converting Europe's
economy to peacetime production. Settle the terms of the
peace, demanded those against tying in the League. Then
we can take up the problem of international organization.

But Wilson, ever suspicious of the motives of the European diplomats, would not agree. He feared that once
Germany had been disarmed it would be impossible to
persuade the Allies to join a league. It can be argued that
his reasoning was unrealistic. What effectiveness would
the League have if its members had to be coerced into
joining? Subsequent history proved that without the
wholehearted support of the great powers the League of
Nations was worse than impotent when international crises developed. This, however, is *ex post facto* reasoning.
Wilson believed that the organization would prove so
useful that the statesmen would quickly recognize its
value, and that public opinion would protect it against
sabotage by cynical politicians.

He had his way, and he was probably right in insist-
ing upon it. While it did take time to fashion the League
Covenant, the overall work on the Versailles Treaty was
expedited rather than held back by its inclusion. Many
touchy problems were settled by compromise or by stop-
gap measures on the assumption that if trouble developed the League could reconsider them. Wilson's mistake lay not in welding the League to the treaty of peace,
but in pinning too much faith on it as a cure-all for the
ills of the world.

All his hopes were in it. He served personally upon
the committee that prepared the final draft, slaving for
hours snatched from his already overburdened schedule,
often laboring late into the night after long days of haggling with Clemenceau and Lloyd George over other aspects of the settlement. Gathered around the table in
Colonel House's office in the Crillon were some of the
most distinguished men at the conference. Wilson presided, flanked by Prime Minister Orlando of Italy and
Colonel House. Next to House sat the British delegates,
General Smuts of South Africa and Lord Robert Cecil,
one of the fathers of the league idea, and beyond them
the French, the Japanese, and the representatives of the
lesser powers. Colonel House's diary provides a picture
of a typical session:

February 7, 1919: We had the usual meeting of
the Committee on the League of Nations last night. We did
not adjourn until eleven. Many important articles were
adopted. Practically everything originates from our end of
the table; that is, with Lord Robert Cecil and the President. . . . The President excels in such work. He seems
to like it and his short talks in explanation of his views are
admirable. I have never known anyone to do such work as
well. The President, perhaps, lays too much stress on de-

tails. It is not a hard-and-fast trade we are making with one another, and a more flexible instrument would be better than a rigid one.

House's criticism (made, as usual, only to his diary) was well taken. By this time Wilson had lost something of his sense of proportion; every word of the Covenant was almost a matter of life or death to him, for the League had become absolutely vital in his eyes. His implacable conscience, tortured by the memory of the thousands who had perished because of his decision to go to war, impelled him to make it so. The victory, won at such a price, must lead to permanent peace. The vengeful selfishness he saw everywhere about him at Paris—the wheedling, petty diplomats, the bloodthirsty editorials in the French papers, the clashing, contentious nationalisms bred of hatred and suspicion—convinced him utterly (and thus beyond compromise) that only through the League of Nations could future wars be avoided.

Later, in the last great speech of his life, he bared the logic that, along with the streak of dogmatism in his personality, explains his uncompromising position when the League was challenged. Time and again, he said (at Pueblo, Colorado, on September 25, 1919), mothers of dead American soldiers had pressed his hand and with tear-filled eyes asked God to bless him. *Why?* Had he not sent their sons to death? "Why should they weep upon my hand and call down the blessings of God upon me?" Because, he explained, "they rightly believe that their sons have saved the liberty of the world." Inextricably wedded to this world freedom, he sternly added, is "the continuous protection of that liberty by the concerted powers of all civilized people."

The combination of Wilson's insistence on specificity

and the need for haste resulted in a Covenant that was far from perfect. The wording in some cases was cumbersome, and there were gaps, such as the failure to provide for a nation's withdrawing from the League if it is so desired. Wilson found it difficult to realize that his handiwork contained flaws, and he resented (and then bitterly resisted) efforts to alter it.

On February 14 Wilson appeared before a plenary session of the Versailles Conference and read his committee's draft to the delegates. The next day he left France for a month. Pressing needs called him back to America. Congress was about to adjourn, and there were bills to sign and routine business to attend to. There was also the task of explaining the League to the people.

Before Wilson left, Colonel House made one of his rare efforts to influence his chief's better judgment. The moment was carefully chosen. House had worked brilliantly over the Covenant and the President was appreciative. When Wilson completed his moving speech at the plenary session, House had passed him a note: "Dear Governor—Your speech was as great as the occasion. I am very happy. EMH." Wilson had scrawled back: "Bless your heart. Thank you from the bottom of my heart. W.W." Now that he was headed home, he placed House in virtual charge of the delegation, bypassing Lansing as usual.

Emboldened by this display of confidence, the Colonel urged Wilson to remember the power of the Senate, and to try to placate the opposition. With great difficulty he persuaded the President to invite the House and Senate leaders to dinner and to seek a meeting of minds with them.

House realized that Wilson underestimated the power of the anti-League senators in both parties. He told him

that he had been "counting noses," and when Wilson
smiled at this, he went into details. Democratic Senator
Hoke Smith of Georgia, for example, was a long-time
enemy of Wilson. They had been rival lawyers in Atlanta, and Smith had never been an administration man
while Wilson was President. "Extend an olive branch to
Hoke Smith," House begged. "If you whistle Hoke will
not come to heel, but if you ask him to come to the
White House and assist you he will come and stay with
you."

"I shall do nothing of the sort!" Wilson replied,
eyes blazing with anger. "That man is an ambulance-
chaser."

"But Governor," House insisted, "this man's vote is
important. . . . If he did chase ambulances thirty
years ago, do not ostracize him. Let him, too, help to
save civilization."

Wilson laughed again, so House pressed him further.
"Governor, I hope you haven't lost your admiration for
Burke. Your essay on that great man was the first product
of your pen that enthralled me."

"Of course not, of course not. When in doubt I always consult Burke or Bagehot or both. But why your
question?"

"Because," House explained, "I recall your Burke
said: 'to govern is to compromise.' "

Wilson laughed once more, but then grew deadly serious. "I know the situation you have in mind, but for
once I do not agree with you or with Burke," he said.
"I have found that you get nothing in this world that is
worth-while without fighting for it."

Thus House knew that he had failed. When Wilson
boarded the boat train at the Paris station, he threw an
arm affectionately round the Colonel's shoulder and

wished him luck, but it was clear that he had not been convinced. House returned to his hotel with Stephen Bonsal, a staff interpreter. "He goes to meet the Senate—" House mused.

"You do not seem hopeful. . . ."

"Hopeful, yes, but not confident. . . ."

X

"I WONDER if you are half as glad to see me as I am to see you." Woodrow Wilson, fresh from Europe, was addressing a packed house in Boston's Mechanics' Hall. Soon he would be in Washington, face to face with a resentful Senate. He had already invited the members of the Congressional committees on foreign affairs to meet with him. Though the draft of the Covenant had been published, he had requested that they refrain from public discussion until he could go over it with them. Yet here he was speaking about the League in advance of the conference, and in Massachusetts, the home of his bitterest critic, Henry Cabot Lodge. "Mr. Wilson has asked me to dinner," Lodge snarled. "[He] also asked me to say nothing. He then goes to my own town and makes a speech—very characteristic."

The President was in a belligerent frame of mind. "America is the hope of the world, and if she does not justify that hope results are unthinkable," he orated. "Any man [the reference to Senator Lodge was unmistakable] who thinks that America will take part in giving the world any such rebuff . . . does not know America. I invite him to test the sentiments of America. . . . I should welcome no sweeter challenge than that. I have fighting blood in me and it is sometimes a delight to let it have scope, but if it is challenged on this occasion it will be an indulgence."

Little wonder that Lodge attended the White House dinner in a sullen and negative mood. But at least he attended. Two members of the Senate Foreign Relations Committee refused even to listen to Wilson's explanation of the Covenant! The dinner was a flat failure, for while Wilson was polite, his resentment was apparent, and the minds of his foes were closed to begin with. The only general agreement that all parties took with them from the table was that nothing had been accomplished. Nothing, that is, except the increased determination of all to stick to their opinions to the last.

The Senate foes of Wilson's League gave the President their formal answer to his plea for support in the dying hours of the Congress. Lodge introduced a resolution, the famous Round Robin, that declared the proposed Covenant unacceptable to the Senate. Discussion would have required unanimous consent, for the resolution was clearly out of order. A Democratic senator refused it. Lodge, expecting and desiring this, did not complain. "I recognize the objection," he said coolly. "I merely wish to add, by way of explanation, the following: 'The undersigned Senators . . . hereby declare that, if they had had the opportunity, they would have voted for the foregoing resolution. . . .'" He then read off a list of thirty-seven names—more than enough to defeat any treaty.

Wilson responded to this challenge with defiance. The next evening he spoke in New York before boarding the *George Washington* to return to France. "An overwhelming majority of the American people is in favor of the League of Nations," he said. "I am amazed—not alarmed but amazed—that there should be in some quarters such a comprehensive ignorance of the state of the world. These gentlemen do not know what the mind of men is just now. . . . When that treaty comes back gentlemen on this side will find the covenant not only in it, but so many threads of the treaty tied to the covenant that you can not dissect the covenant from the treaty without destroying the whole vital structure." In private

he said to Senator Martin of Virginia, who had warned
of the problem presented by the Round Robin: "Martin!
Anyone who opposes me in that, I'll crush!"

Wilson returned to the Versailles Conference embittered and stubborn. House, meeting him at Brest, noticed that he had come back "very militant and determined to put the League of Nations into the Peace
Treaty." What the President found at Paris did not
lighten his mood. Great progress had been made in working out the military and territorial aspects of the settlement, but in the process the League had been pushed
into the background. There was talk of a preliminary
treaty that would disarm the enemy and parcel out the
spoils, saving discussion of the League for a "permanent"
treaty afterwards. Wilson believed that this would endan-
ger all his hopes. What assurance could he have that
with immediate needs satisfied, the Allies (and especially
the United States Senate) would ever agree to set up the
League? At once he issued a statement that repudiated
the idea of a preliminary pact, and there is some evidence
that he was quite irritated by House's "compromises"
during his absence.

Wilson's temper was further inflamed by irresistible
pressures that had built up for a reconsideration of some
of the clauses in the Covenant. Perhaps the Senate did
not understand the modern world; perhaps it did not re-
flect public feeling. But even more enlightened and
friendly Americans were raising objections to certain
parts of the plan. Realizing that if the subject were re-
opened the European powers would also have revisions
to suggest, he resisted reconvening the committee on the
League, but finally gave in.

He was forced to effect four changes. Two were unexceptionable: a proviso that no nation had to accept a

colonial mandate from the League, and one that exempted "domestic questions" (to Americans this meant particularly immigration controls and tariffs) from League control. The other two caused great difficulty.

Of these the first concerned the Monroe Doctrine. American opinion was demanding that the revered and hoary Doctrine be specifically recognized in the Covenant. President Monroe had "closed" the Western Hemisphere to further colonization in 1823. Though this policy had never received international recognition, it was as much a part of the American political system as the Constitution, and public opinion insisted that its restrictions be written into the treaty. Wilson thought this unnecessary. To him the League merely extended to the rest of the world the protection that the United States had offered its American neighbors, and made it reciprocal. But unnecessary or not, it had to be, and Wilson manfully asked the Committee on the League to accept an amendment mentioning the Doctrine by name and excluding it from the jurisdiction of the League.

The other alteration seemed petty, but caused much trouble. There was no provision in the Covenant whereby a member of the League could withdraw from the organization. Responding to pressure from home, Wilson urged that a two-year "escape" clause be added. This brought vehement protests from the French, who felt that whatever security the League might afford would be destroyed if members could withdraw so easily. Wilson depreciated this danger. No state would ever have a *moral* right to abandon the League, he argued, only a legal right. This was not the only time he was to draw this abstruse distinction. Further, no state would ever *want* to withdraw. "One of my difficulties," he explained, "is that Americans demand complete assurance that they are not being called upon to give up [their] sovereignty. . . . The day is near when they will become as eager partisans of the sovereignty of mankind as they are now of their national or State sovereignty. But, for the moment, it is necessary to take into consideration current prejudices."

Wilson obtained all these concessions, but at great price. The French pressed him unmercifully. "You come over here," one delegate shouted at him, "and dictate what we should do and what we should not do, and yet you do not let us have our say as to what you propose doing over there!" If the League was to be weakened, Wilson must agree to French occupation of the Rhineland as protection against Germany. This was mere politicking, however. Far more serious was the effect that Wilson's requests had on liberal opinion. "We were told that the word Covenant connoted something sacramental," that it had "the sanction of God," Colonel Bonsal quoted Paris liberals as saying. "Now it appears it is only binding for twenty-four months." A liberal editor thundered: "We must look our situation straight in the eye unpleasant as it is. We are confronted with the complete failure of . . . the one man in whom we put our confidence." True enough, the other leaders were far worse. "Of them, however, we expected nothing. . . . One and all we knew them to be insignificant hypocrites. But Wilson—"

These attacks were unfair, except in the sense that Wilson was in part responsible for the unrealistically high hopes that such liberals had entertained. In accepting the "escape" clause, Wilson was not compromising any essential principle, and was doing even what he did with the greatest reluctance. But, coming as it did along with other concessions, it injured Wilson's prestige.

As March turned into April the conference entered its blackest period. Everywhere selfish national interests threatened the peace of justice. The Big Four at last had come to grips with the vital questions—the Franco-German border and Italy's northern frontier, the difficult problem of reparations, the future of Germany's sphere of influence in China's Shantung peninsula. A truly titanic struggle developed over the coal-rich Saar area, which France wished to wrest from Germany. The Germans had exploited French mines during the war, and then destroyed them in their retreat. The French demanded the Saar as compensation. But the Saar was overwhelmingly German. Wilson would not agree to any such violation of the principle of national self-determination.

In this he clashed head-on with Clemenceau. The Tiger pointed out that France had held the area under Napoleon. That, Wilson reminded him, had been a hundred years ago, a very long time. "A very long time in the history of the United States," Clemenceau snapped.

So heated did the discussions become that Clemenceau finally stalked out of a meeting in a huff. When friends urged him to continue the talks he said with great indignation: "Talk with Wilson! How can I talk to a fellow who thinks himself the first man in two thousand years to know anything about peace on earth?"

The strain on Wilson mounted constantly. Personal conflict was always difficult for him. At the same time his work revising the League kept him up late night after night, denying him the sleep that was so essential to his health. By late March it was clear to those around him that he was a sick man. He developed a chronic tic that distorted the left side of his face; he grew peevish and nervous. Even Clemenceau expressed concern for his condition, and another French diplomat told Colonel House: "What we fear is that the President is near a physical breakdown."

On April 3, quite suddenly, he was taken violently ill. His temperature shot up to 103; he suffered severe paroxysms of coughing that made breathing difficult, combined with diarrhea. The symptoms were so violent that at first his physician, Doctor Cary Grayson, suspected that he had been poisoned. The poor doctor spent a terrible night trying to control them. Eventually he changed his diagnosis to influenza, and the press was informed that the President was suffering from a cold.

It is impossible to say at this date exactly what had happened, but it is probable that Wilson had a slight stroke. He had been afflicted for years with arteriosclerosis. In 1906 he lost the sight of his left eye for a time as a result of a mild attack. His physician had then warned him: "You were fortunate in having the local trouble because it called attention to the general condition. . . . The warning simply indicates that excess of work is dangerous." Wilson was incapable of following this advice for any extended period, and increasing age aggravated his condition. The strains he underwent at Paris, which might have crushed a healthy man half his age, were more than his system could stand.

Even so, he staged a remarkable recovery, and the importance of the attack might seem small but for its psychological implications. Minor strokes (which often pass unrecognized) can produce significant changes in a man's personality without actually impairing his intellectual equipment to any noticeable degree. These changes vary from individual to individual. Sometimes they involve moral disintegration, which was certainly not true in Wilson's case. Frequently they cause emotional hyperactivity, irascibility, depression, or a feeling of persecution. There tends to be a decline in judgment and an increase in stubbornness. None of these symptoms *necessarily* occurs, and usually the victim has long periods of complete "normality" punctuated by brief outbursts of untypical behavior. It is therefore difficult to make a positive diagnosis of Wilson's case. But there is much evidence indicating that his attack was caused by the rupture of a small inter-cranial artery.

It may even be that the Paris attack was preceded by others of lesser force. Ray Stannard Baker noted that as early as 1916 "it was easier for him to become irritated, if not angry," than in earlier days. Baker attributed this to "the violent emotions generated by the war," but the medical explanation may be more reasonable. At least two doctors, one of whom had known him from boyhood, noticed subtle changes in Wilson's character and attributed them to arteriosclerosis. In any case, after he recovered from the April seizure, many persons observed a distinct change in his personality. "Prior to that time," Herbert Hoover recalled in his *Memoirs*, "he was incisive, quick to grasp essentials, unhesitating in conclusions. . . . After the time I mention . . . I found that we had to push against an unwilling mind." "Mr. Wilson never seemed the same to his associates," a correspondent observed. Secretary Lansing perhaps saw the situation backward when he wrote that "certain traits of his character, which had been so prominent in his public career prior to that time, seem to have been suppressed or submerged in the new environment" of Paris, but his comment too illustrates that Wilson *changed*.

While Wilson was ill the Big Four continued to meet, with Colonel House representing his chief. The question of the Saar continued to plague them, as well as the

French refusal to set a fixed limit upon the amount of reparations to be exacted from the enemy. One by one House brought compromise solutions to Wilson's bedside only to have them rejected. At one point the President became so exasperated that he threatened to quit the conference and ask Congress to make a separate peace with Germany. Undoubtedly this helped persuade Clemenceau to moderate his claims, but in the end Wilson also made concessions, although, as House said, he did so with "a wry face." France got the Saar for fifteen years, with a plebiscite to follow which would settle permanent ownership of the region. On reparations the French view prevailed, but although no definite sum was set, a Reparations Commission was given broad authority to determine a fair settlement at some later date.

As soon as he was up and about, Wilson resumed his labors, and gradually the Versailles Treaty assumed its final shape. When it was finished in May, hopeful liberals stacked it up against the Fourteen Points upon which it was supposed to be based, and were shocked by what they saw.

"When I read the first proofs of the Treaty," so sympathetic a man as Ray Stannard Baker recalled, "it seemed to me a terrible document; a dispensation of retribution with scarcely a parallel in history." Herbert Hoover, roused at four in the morning by a messenger bearing a copy of the document, read it at once. "Hate and revenge ran through the political and economic passages," he wrote. Profoundly disturbed, he dressed and went out to pace the empty streets of Paris. Soon he met General Smuts of South Africa and the British economist, John Maynard Keynes. They were equally depressed. "We agreed that it was terrible and we would do what we could among our own nationals to make the

dangers clear." Keynes in particular took this pledge to
heart; his *The Economic Consequences of the Peace* was
a denunciation of the Treaty and one of the most influential books of the post-war era.

These men, and others like them, were appalled by
the violations of the Fourteen Points they found in the
Treaty. It was perhaps an open covenant, but it had certainly not been openly arrived at. Freedom of the seas
was not even mentioned, and nothing had been done to
foster free trade or speed world disarmament. It was difficult, despite the establishment of the mandate system,
to see how the welfare of the native peoples in Germany's
former colonies was being served by turning them over
to the imperialist mercies of England, France, Italy, and
Japan. And what of self-determination? The Treaty put
German Saarlanders under the heel of a vindictive
France, drove a wedge of Polish territory from Silesia to
the Baltic across people predominantly German, and
placed thousands of Austrians in the South Tyrol under
the Italian flag. Germany was to sign a blank check in
payment of a bill that would include pensions for Allied
soldiers as well as compensation for legitimate damages,
and Woodrow Wilson, the man who had expressed such
profound doubts about the causes of the war, was now
requiring the Germans to admit their sole guilt for all
the death and destruction the war had wrought. Was this
peace without victory? Was this the foundation stone on
which international friendship and human good will were
to build a better world?

That the Fourteen Points had been "violated" was apparent. That Wilson had sacrificed principle to expediency on a number of occasions was beyond argument.
That he had sometimes erred in his dealings with the
other statesmen was also clear. It was less obvious that

he had worked against great odds. A regiment of super-
men could not have reordered tangled Europe in a manner satisfactory to all. And who could deny that he had
achieved many remarkable successes along with his failures?

Above all he had made his League of Nations. Freedom of the seas would no longer be a problem if an international congress of nations could preserve universal
peace. Clemenceau had said that war would not be war
if there was freedom of the seas. Wilson could have retorted that the seas would always be free if there were no
wars. Disarmament would be simple once the League
had proved itself, and the relaxation of trade barriers
would surely follow. The mandate system was at least in
principle a victory over the forces of imperialism.

As to self-determination, perfection was impossible in
the welter of Europe, but certainly the new boundaries
left fewer people on "foreign" soil than ever before (or
since) in the history of the continent. Winston Churchill estimated that less than three per cent of the population would have preferred to live under a different flag
after 1919.

Before he left Paris for good, Wilson held a mass interview at the Crillon for the newspapermen. The well-
known radical journalist, Lincoln Steffens, was present,
disillusioned and disgusted by the Treaty. "Mr. President," he asked, "do you feel that you achieved here the
peace that you expected to make?" Wilson looked
squarely at him. He spoke slowly, carefully, earnestly: "I
think we have made a better peace than I should have
expected when I came here to Paris." Steffens was outraged; he felt that the President had abandoned all integrity. But Wilson was sincere. On the *George Washington*, as he first approached the shores of France, he had

discussed the awful problems that lay ahead with George Creel. "These ancient wrongs . . . are not to be remedied in a day or with a wave of the hand," he said. "What I seem to see—with all my heart I hope that I am wrong—is a tragedy of disappointment." He was also justified in praising the Treaty.

It is true that much depended upon the League of Nations. Wilson was convinced that the League was "the key to peace," completely transcending the specific settlements of Paris, which were essentially temporary adjustments of immediate problems. His critics have argued that this feeling amounted to an obsession. Harold Nicolson said it reflected the President's "inner insecurity." Another contemporary wrote:

Wilson's interest in the League idea . . . spread like a tree until it overshadowed all else. . . . Intellectual infatuation . . . and his own pacifist obsession combined to make this consummation inevitable. If a League of Nations could be reared upon the ruins of the World War, then no price in blood was too high to pay. A League . . . was the only achievement that justified Wilson the warrior before his own Scotch-Presbyterian conscience.

John Maynard Keynes even believed that Wilson's satisfaction with the whole Versailles Treaty was one vast rationalization designed to protect his conscience against guilt-feelings rising from his sacrifice of the Fourteen Points. "To suggest to the President that the Treaty was an abandonment of his professions was to touch on the raw a Freudian complex," Keynes wrote in *The Economic Consequences of the Peace*. "It was a subject intolerable to discuss, and every subconscious instinct plotted to defeat its further exploration."

There is probably much truth in these analyses. But a

man can rationalize and still be right; he can be obsessed and still be objectively correct. Emotion may have governed Wilson's thinking, but logic was on his side as well.

However, no matter how correct, rigid conviction is unsuited to the bargaining table. Wilson came back to the United States in 1919 with a better treaty than many intelligent men had ever expected to see, and with powerful weapons to defend it. But he did not employ these weapons effectively.

Wilson's one objective after his return to America was to persuade two thirds of the United States Senate to ratify the Treaty. Nearly all the Democratic senators could be counted on to follow his leadership, but since less than half of the Senate was Democratic, he would have to obtain many Republican votes to accomplish his purpose. There were two ways of doing this. One was to apply all the instruments of Presidential persuasion. He could appeal to the senators' patriotism, bribe them with patronage, convince them with argument, engage in political "horse-trading" with them, and make concessions in the form of amendments or reservations to the Treaty to bring it more in line with their thinking, giving them an excuse for saying that their party too had shared in fashioning the agreement. Wilson tried all these techniques except the last, but in a halfhearted manner.

The alternative approach was to bring to bear upon the senators the power of public opinion and the logic of events so forcefully that they would have to support the Treaty whether they liked it or not. Everything combined to make Wilson follow this course. His intense conviction of the value of the Treaty was reinforced by his distaste, after the endless quibbles and quarrels of

Paris, for further bargaining and compromise. His basic nature—his dislike of dealing in personalities, his tendency to see things in absolute terms, his tenacity over questions of principle, and his abhorrence of compromise where moral issues were involved—combined with his recently exaggerated stubbornness and irascibility to make this strategy appealing.

Always in crises he liked to place his faith in the people, for he had complete confidence in his ability to reach them and bring them to his side. Conversely, he viewed the Senate with intense suspicion. As a powerful executive, he was frequently in conflict with congressmen, and most often with senators, who tend to be jealous of their prerogatives and independence. The intemperate criticisms of many senators while the Treaty was being hammered into shape had stirred him deeply. "Those Senators do not know what the people are thinking," he said after reading an editorial commenting upon the resistance of the Upper House to the League of Nations. "They are as far from the people, the great mass of our people, as I am from Mars. . . . Naturally they cannot understand them." The Round Robin made him still angrier. To go before these men with an expectant and cajoling smile, to plead, wheedle, explain, debate, threaten, or argue them into supporting the Treaty was repugnant to him.

A direct appeal to the people could also be defended on practical grounds. The masses were certainly for the Treaty and the League, in principle at least. Even Senator Lodge admitted that "a large majority of the people of the country are very naturally fascinated by the idea of eternal preservation of the world's peace." They were still more eager to see the war officially ended. Wilson had cleverly made what would today be called a "package deal" of the Treaty and the League. It was impossible to accept one without the other. With the public favoring an international organization dedicated to the prevention of war, and wanting to bring the soldiers home as quickly as possible, the Senate would not dare to reject the one means of accomplishing both (or either) of these objectives. The bold senator who might consider flouting the popular will could be brought to heel by the sharp command of his constituents. A few inspiring speeches by the President, mustering the people against unpatriotic, selfish politicians, would precipitate a flood of angry mail upon Capitol Hill, and float the Treaty to safe harbor.

Wilson's strategy, then, was ruthless but not illogical. It failed not because it was ill-conceived, but because the President refused to modify it to meet the changing conditions of the developing battle. Instead of resorting to maneuver when difficulties arose, instead of backtracking or sidestepping when his clever and unscrupulous opponents laid ambushes in his path, he charged courageously but stubbornly forward like the Light Brigade at Balaklava to heroic but tragically unnecessary defeat.

Wilson's foes in the Senate quickly accepted his defiant challenge. The opposition was roughly divided into three factions, but each rose to the occasion in its particular way. The extremists were ready to fight the President on his own terms. These "irreconcilables" were led by William E. Borah of Idaho, able, kindly, a brilliant orator of progressive views, but uncompromisingly isolationist and almost congenitally predisposed to oppose the will of powerful executives. Borah claimed that he would vote against the League even if Jesus Christ returned to earth to argue in its behalf, and most of his dozen-odd followers were equally stubborn.

The moderates, men like Porter J. McCumber and

Charles L. McNary, favored the League substantially as Wilson had fashioned it, desiring only "mild reservations" guaranteeing certain American rights. The difference between these senators and the third faction was only one of degree. This group demanded "strong" reservations. They approved, or at least were willing to tolerate, the *idea* of a league of nations, but would not accept Wilson's League unless substantial changes were made. Senator Lodge was spokesman for the strong reservationists, and as majority leader of the Senate, was the titular head of the other groups as well.

Had Wilson been adaptable and conciliatory he could have won the moderates and many of the Lodge faction for his cause; instead, by his rigidity and hostility he unified the opposition and contributed to his own defeat. He played right into the hands of his enemy, Lodge. As majority leader, the Senator had an almost impossible task to perform. His party was badly split over the League, yet with a presidential election forthcoming, it was his job to maintain a solid front. He labored assiduously and displayed real brilliance as a parliamentary manager, but without Wilson's goading he could never have kept his team in harness.

The different tactics of Lodge and Wilson are most revealing. Lodge was all flexibility in dealing with his fellow senators. He persuaded Borah to help in passing reservations that would lessen American obligations under the League when the Idaho Senator's impulse was to vote against anything connected with the Treaty. He held the mild reservationists in line by modifying some of his own demands and by preaching the virtues of party regularity. One day he was sweet reasonableness itself to the friends of the League; the next he was allowing himself to be "intimidated" by the isolationists in the G.O.P.

One of his enemies remarked afterward that to follow his path through the League fight would have broken the back of a rattlesnake.

Wilson, however, would do nothing to make it easier for his political opponents to support the League. The Republicans naturally wanted some of the credit for saving the world, for if the Democrats could pose as the sole sponsors of world peace they would have a valuable advantage in the coming election. It was too late to give the Republicans a share in formulating the plan, but if they could be credited with a few minor revisions, they would be more inclined to forget the political implications and act on their consciences. But Wilson would not help them at all.

This might have been justified if Wilson's major premise—that the people were overwhelmingly in favor of the League of Nations—had been correct. Unfortunately for him, it was not entirely so. Most people seemed favorably disposed toward the general idea, but few had any strong convictions about every clause in the Covenant. Still more important, many Americans had not considered fully all the implications of joining an international organization. As the enemies of the League developed their arguments in public debate, the basic changes in American thinking that membership would involve became gradually apparent. Traditional isolationism and nationalism, along with suspicion of foreigners, distrust of European diplomacy, and other unlovely aspects of the American mind, were brought to the fore.

The irreconcilables played on every passion to defeat the League. Foreign diplomats would be able to send American soldiers to die on distant shores; the British Empire would have six votes to one for the United

States; tiny Liberia would be equal in influence to mighty America. Some of these charges were merely silly, some were plain lies, but they affected the thinking of many people. And the most thoughtful citizen, examining the evidence, found it difficult to object to some of the changes suggested by the Republicans. When Wilson refused to make any concessions, the charges of the extremists that he was egotistical, dictatorial, and partisan began to take effect. The passage of time added further to the strength of the League's foes.

No one appreciated the importance of time more fully than Senator Lodge. Lodge hated the President, and was convinced that his stubborn refusal to modify the League sprang from mere egotism. Privately he referred to Wilson as "El Supremo." He believed that Wilson's ultimate objective was a third term; his own was certainly the frustration of this ambition and the election of a Republican.

As chairman of the Foreign Relations Committee, Lodge had charge of the Treaty in the Senate. First he consumed two weeks of hearings by reading the entire text of the long Treaty aloud. Then he called for witnesses. Some, like Secretary Lansing, had real information to give if they would, but many others were merely representatives of minority groups who used the hearings to vent their wrath against whatever aspects of the Treaty they disliked. Lodge, for example, blandly permitted the friends of Irish independence to state their case before the Committee though the Treaty was not even remotely concerned with the Irish problem. Lodge also badgered the President with requests for papers and documents, which Wilson refused to turn over whenever possible. The haughty, supercilious, acid-tongued Senator was an expert at infuriating his foes. Wilson became so incensed

that his secretary had to intervene to keep him from being rude and petulant in his answers to Lodge's studi-
ously polite letters.

Wilson did not refuse to discuss the Covenant with
his opponents. Under pressure from his advisers he summoned a number of Republican senators to the White
House for individual conferences. But all he would do
was explain; he was unwilling to heed their suggestions,
although almost to a man they informed him that his
Treaty would fail unless reservations were added limiting
America's obligations to the League. One senator told
him frankly that his only chance lay in accepting the so-
called Lodge "strong" reservations. Wilson bristled. "Accept the Treaty with the *Lodge* reservations," he snorted.
"Never! Never! . . . I'll appeal to the country!"

At last this was what he did. By the end of the summer he was desperately tired. Besides the burden of the
League he had been forced to deal with a host of domestic problems. As soon as the armistice was signed, all
wartime controls were relaxed and the economy left to
shift for itself in the reconversion period. The result was
shortages, skyrocketing prices, and social unrest. Strikes
convulsed the textile, communications, and railroad in-
dustries, while in the summer of 1919 newly organized
steel workers prepared for a showdown with their anti-
union employers. Radicalism was on the rise, stimulated
by the success of the Russian Revolution, producing besides isolated cases of violence an inevitable reaction of
unbridled "red-hunting." Race riots flared from Texas to
Illinois; lynchings increased in number. Wilson struggled with all these problems at the same time that he
fought his great battle with the Senate, and they took
their toll of his failing strength.

But the League was worth any sacrifice. Early in September he decided to make a speaking tour through the West to present his case to the people. Dr. Grayson warned him that he was not well enough; Mrs. Wilson was apprehensive. In the middle of August he had endured a long grilling by the Foreign Relations Committee in which he made repeatedly the startling statement that he had never heard of the notorious secret treaties concluded by the Allies with Italy and Japan until after his arrival in Paris. This was so obviously untrue—the provisions of some of the treaties had been published in American newspapers a year before Wilson's departure —that his action can only be explained in terms of loss of memory, an ominous sign. But Wilson was determined. Perhaps he was actually in search of martyrdom, ready to make the ultimate sacrifice to save his League of Nations. "It is my duty," he told Grayson. "My own health is not to be considered when the future peace and security of the world is at stake. . . . I must go."

On September 3, accompanied by Mrs. Wilson, Joe Tumulty, Dr. Grayson, and a trainful of reporters, secretaries, and secret service men, he set out for the West.

XI

THE *Presidential Special* roared through the night across Maryland and over the Appalachians to Columbus, Ohio. In the morning, Wilson drove to Memorial Hall through rain-washed streets to give "the only people I owe any report to" an account of the Treaty and the Covenant. The grueling tour of the West had begun.

From Columbus the President pushed on to Indianapolis and then across the rich Illinois prairies to St. Louis and Kansas City. Then he moved north in a zigzag path, amid the cornfields of Iowa and Nebraska, to Minneapolis and St. Paul; then west again through the wheatlands of the northern tier, across Montana and Borah's Idaho to Seattle; then south to California. From San Francisco to Los Angeles to San Diego the President rolled on; speaking in auditoriums and great stadia, and from the rear platform of his train, he addressed city crowds and knots of farmers clustered at the whistle-stops. But always he spoke to the people, the masses who must save his Treaty and his League. Onward, ever onward he pressed, now eastward over the passes to the Great Salt Lake and the Mormon Tabernacle, to Cheyenne, to Denver, to Pueblo. . . .

Three weeks passed with scarcely a moment of quiet or rest. Noise and movement were the themes of the journey. Consider for a moment the sounds: the mighty roar of fifty thousand voices responding to Wilson at the San Diego Stadium; the blare and boom of parading bands; the oily periods of countless local chairmen introducing "the President of the United States"; the demanding voices of a hundred reporters, pencils poised, minds on today's ball game; the senseless shriek of a solitary heckler. Add to these the unending rumble of the heavy cars, the locomotive's mournful warning at a thousand grade-crossings, the clatter and click of steel wheels over mile upon mile of track. And at night, between Sioux Falls and St. Paul, between Helena and Coeur d'Alene, the tapping keys of the President's typewriter.

Now visualize the ever-changing scene: lines of children waving little American flags; fat, sweating politicians in high silk hats and rented cutaways, waiting expectantly at rural stations and city terminals for a chance to shake the hand of a man greater than themselves and pose with false smiles for the photographers; boy scouts, policemen, and grim-faced secret-service agents holding back straining crowds as the presidential party squeezes past; clouds of torn paper fluttering down indiscriminately from office buildings onto the shoulders of parading dignitaries and close-packed observers; the constant rush of telegraph poles, ever retreating into the past; the sudden red blur of signal lights in the night; the majesty of distant mountains framed in the windows of the moving train.

Wilson spoke under all kinds of conditions. Sometimes the halls were far from full, sometimes they were jammed to the doors. In Seattle seats changed hands for as much as twenty-five dollars. In Indianapolis he spoke at the fair grounds and had to compete with prize Indiana livestock for the crowd's attention. His reception was also varied. Nowhere was he received with hostility, but sometimes the crowds were apathetic to his impassioned pleas. At other times his eloquence brought forth sustained ovations—even tears. His message also differed as he moved from place to place. His early speeches were explanatory and confidently cool. He stressed abstractions like justice, morality, generosity, and duty. Later he became more earnest and emotional. The emphasis switched from the Treaty in general to the League in particular; uncomplimentary references to the Senate opposition also became more frequent. Several times he demanded, with a colloquialism unsuited to his personality, that his enemies "put up or shut up"—suggest a better League or accept the one he had fashioned.

He made errors too, both of fact and tactics. His speeches, despite some brilliant paragraphs, were not among his best. Yet without a staff of researchers and ghost writers, and in the face of diminishing vitality, he maintained his schedule day after day. And for speeches largely extemporaneous they were remarkably good. Worn down by fatigue, tortured by relentless headaches, so ill that he could seldom eat more than a few mouthfuls, he seemed time and again on the point of collapse. But when the moment came to rise from his chair, the sea of expectant faces gave him, as always, new strength.

As the tour passed the mid-point, when Wilson might have been expected to take heart at the thought of its approaching end, his condition grew worse instead of better. Dr. Grayson and Mrs. Wilson watched him anxiously. After his moving speech at Pueblo, Colorado, as the train pushed on toward Wichita, he reached the end of his resources. In desperation Dr. Grayson ordered the train stopped for half an hour so that the President could take a walk in the cool Colorado countryside. Afterward he felt a little better. But that night, as she was preparing for bed, Mrs. Wilson was interrupted by a knock on her door. It was Wilson. He could not sleep; the pain in his head was unbearable. Dr. Grayson was summoned at once.

Mrs. Wilson has left a graphic picture of the President in his night clothes, sitting on the side of his bed in the swaying compartment, resting his tortured head on the back of a chair. "That night was the longest and most heartbreaking of my life," she wrote. "Nothing the Doctor could do gave relief. Finally the President got up and dressed. He said he could not stay in that tiny room; he must move about." At five o'clock he fell asleep at last, sitting bolt-upright on a straight chair. He awoke two hours later, doggedly determined to prepare for his Wichita speech. The doctor, Mrs. Wilson, and Joe Tumulty combined to persuade him to give it up. "No, no, no," he protested. "I must keep on." But finally he realized that it was impossible. The news went out to a shocked and puzzled nation. The President was ill; the remainder of the speeches were canceled.

Two days later the train reached Washington. A large crowd was on hand, and Wilson managed to walk briskly through the terminal and to pose for the photographers before returning to the White House. There was a great deal of speculation as to his condition. He remained up and about, but the headaches continued unabated. As he had feared, his enemies accused him of "quitting." Then on October 2 all doubts were removed. When Mrs. Wilson went to his room that morning she found him groping feebly for a water bottle on his bedside stand. His left arm hung loosely. "I have no feeling in that hand," he told her weakly. "Will you rub it?" Gingerly Mrs. Wilson helped her limping, pain-wracked husband to the bathroom. Then she hurried to phone Dr. Grayson. While they talked she heard a muffled thump in the bathroom. She rushed back to find Wilson sprawled unconscious on the floor. He had suffered a stroke.

For two weeks he was on the verge of death. His left side was partially paralyzed; digestive difficulties and a prostate condition added complications. The White

House was full of doctors and nurses. Yet no hint of his true condition was given to the public.

During this critical period Mrs. Wilson was for practical purposes the President of the United States. For another six weeks she, along with Dr. Grayson, exerted more influence over the office than Wilson himself, for their decisions determined what business was brought to his attention. Indeed, for the remainder of his term Mrs. Wilson acted as a buffer between her husband and the duties of his office in a way scarcely contemplated by the Constitution.

She did so with the best of intentions. She labored diligently, thoughtfully, tenderly, and with an awareness of her important responsibilities. But her work was not in the public interest. For (understandably enough) she was primarily a wife and only secondarily a public servant. When a group of harried officials demanded to see the President on an urgent matter of state, she told them coolly: "I am not interested in the President of the United States. I am interested in my husband and his health."

Friends of the administration have stressed the services she performed, and her loyalty to Wilson in his time of need. "Mrs. Wilson . . . impressed me again with her good sense, her real understanding of the difficulties of the present situation, and her eagerness to help," Ray Stannard Baker noted. Tumulty recalled in *Woodrow Wilson as I Know Him*: "Her high intelligence and her extraordinary memory enabled her to report to him daily, in lucid detail, weighty matters of state brought to her by officials for transmission to him. . . . When he was least in pain and least exhausted, she would present a clear, oral résumé of each case." But Tumulty also admitted that Dr. Grayson and Mrs. Wilson had warned him "not to alarm [the President] unduly by bringing pessimistic reports" to his attention. Tumulty sometimes disregarded this advice, but his own love of his chief often kept him from telling Wilson the whole truth about Washington developments. As a result Wilson was uninformed and misinformed on many critical matters. The government had no real head; Cabinet members ran their own Departments, aided only by an occasional cryptic note scrawled across memoranda they had submitted to the White House.

Even when Wilson had recovered enough to meet with his administrators, these men were always made aware of the danger of worrying or overstimulating him. Secretary Houston told a correspondent of one conference at which Mrs. Wilson, her brow furrowed with concern, suddenly appeared in the doorway. "I do not recall that she made any communication," Houston said. "[But] it was not difficult for us . . . to sense her solicitude. Soon thereafter the President adjourned the meeting."

It would have been better if the stroke had killed the President outright. He would have been spared much pain and frustration, and the nation a long period of bitter partisan conflict. Probably the Senate would then have ratified the Treaty with only minor alterations, and America would have entered the League. As it was, Wilson recovered slowly, but never regained his full strength. Seldom again was he able to work more than an hour or two a day. Invalidism added to the querulousness and emotional instability occasioned by arterial deterioration. He was frequently melancholy to the point of tears; he brooded, then flared angrily at his foes. His stubbornness grew to unreasoning proportions. He was never irrational, but his judgment was no longer reliable. His illusions became delusions.

During the first year of the war he had complained to

his daughter of the burdens of his great office. "I am surprisingly well," he told her, "though *very* tired all the time. I am very thankful. I do not see how any but a well man could safely be trusted to decide anything in the present circumstances." Now, alas, he was no longer capable of acting on this wise judgment. When his physicians hinted that he should resign, he disregarded them. Instead, he evolved a fantastic scheme whereby the opposition senators would resign in a body so that an election could be held to test public sentiment on the League issue. Most incredible of all, he toyed repeatedly with the idea of running for a third term.

While the President lay in the White House, the struggle in the Senate moved toward a climax. The Foreign Relations Committee had reported the Treaty out with amendments and reservations while Wilson was stumping the West. The amendments, which would have required resubmission of the Treaty to the other powers, were defeated in the full Senate, but the reservations, fourteen of them eventually, were carried by an almost solid Republican vote, buttressed by the help of a few Democratic irreconcilables.

These "Lodge Reservations" did not alter the Covenant in any fundamental way. Some were unnecessary, some dictated by partisan spite; most of them were designed to define more clearly America's obligations under the League and make certain that Congress would have the final say when the League called upon the United States to meet these obligations. One reservation stated that the United States could not accept a colonial mandate unless Congress approved. A second made more concrete Congress's power to decide what was a "domestic question" and thus outside the authority of the

League. Others stated America's unwillingness to have
the Monroe Doctrine interpreted by foreign powers,
made Congress the sole judge of when America could
honorably withdraw from the organization, and established similar checks on such matters as disarmament and
reparations.

The most important reservation applied to Article X
of the League charter. Wilson called Article X "the
heart of the Covenant." It read:

The members of the League undertake to respect and preserve as against external aggression the territorial integrity
and existing political independence of all Members of the
League. . . . The Council shall advise upon the means by
which this obligation shall be fulfilled.

The reservation to Article X said that it would not apply
to the United States "unless in any particular case the
Congress, which . . . has the sole power to declare
war or authorize the employment of the military or naval
forces of the United States, shall by act or joint resolution so provide."

No doubt these reservations were conceived in a mean
and petty spirit. But at least they dealt forthrightly with
the problem of reconciling nationalism with world co-
operation. Without the reservation to Article X, for example, Congress could prevent American participation
in any international police action through its control of
the purse. Wilson himself admitted as much; his differ-
entiation between a legal and a moral obligation was
based on his recognition that Congress actually had the
final say. A good case can be made for the proposition
that it was better to spell out the full truth than to create
a false impression of American attitudes in foreign minds.

But this consideration aside, by November 1919 it

was a political fact that the Treaty could not pass without the reservations. Before his stroke Wilson had been
willing to consider interpretive reservations provided
they were not actually incorporated into the Treaty.
Nothing had come of this idea, partly because Wilson
had stiffened his attitude in the face of criticism, partly
because after his collapse he was unable to see congressional leaders. His Democratic followers in the Senate
were confused and rudderless. Almost to a man they
wanted to compromise with the reservationists, yet they
could get no word from the White House authorizing
them to do so.

Finally, in November, the minority leader, Senator
Gilbert Hitchcock of Nebraska, was allowed to talk with
the President. Wilson was in bed. He had grown a
beard, which was snowy white, to mask his gaunt and
twisted face. The Senator tried to explain that ratification was impossible without reservations, but explanation was difficult. Mrs. Wilson and Dr. Grayson were at
hand to make sure that the patient was not unduly upset,
yet how to tell him the truth without upsetting him?
When Hitchcock mentioned that the Democrats lacked
the votes to carry the Treaty, Wilson groaned. "Is it possible," he cried. "Is it possible!" He did not seem to realize that conditions had changed since his collapse.

Hitchcock was desperate. He did not want to hurt
Wilson, but he knew that unless he disillusioned him
the Treaty would fail. "Mr. President," he said at last,
"it might be wise to compromise with Lodge."

The mere mention of the name of his enemy made
Wilson see red. "Let Lodge compromise," he snapped.

"Well, of course, he must compromise also," Hitchcock quickly admitted. "But we might well hold out the
olive branch."

"Let Lodge hold out the olive branch."

There was nothing to do. Mrs. Wilson and the doctor were growing restive. Hopelessly, the Senator abandoned the argument.

The day of decision was approaching rapidly. Only Wilson could now save the Treaty, and he refused to do so. From every side came pleas for compromise. He was deaf to them all. Colonel House, ever active on the fringes of great events, sent a friend to dicker with Lodge. Lodge reportedly sketched out his minimum demands on a copy of the Covenant. These House posted to Wilson. The President did not even answer House's letter. Perhaps House's handling of affairs at the Peace Conference had irritated him—there had been rumors of a "break" between the two for months. Perhaps he felt the suggestion of a deal with Lodge to be "disloyal." Perhaps he never read the letter—Mrs. Wilson did not like House, and may well have kept it from him. In any case the letter was ignored. House never saw his friend alive again.

On November 19 the Senate voted. The day before, Mrs. Wilson herself had begged the President to give in. "For my sake," she asked, "won't you accept these reservations and get this awful thing settled?" Wilson turned his head on his pillow, and reaching out, took her hand in his. "Little girl, don't you desert me," he said. "That I cannot stand. . . . It is not *I* that will not accept; it is the Nation's honour that is at stake." Then he added with deep conviction: "Better a thousand times to go down fighting than to dip your colours to dishonourable compromise."

Thus defeat was inevitable. First the Democrats defeated the Treaty with the Lodge reservations. Then the Republicans defeated it without them.

Friends of the League in both parties did not give up

hope. Compromise suggestions appeared from many quarters, and public opinion forced the Senate to reconsider the Treaty in the early months of 1920. But there was never a real chance of passing it, for both the principals were unwilling to budge. "The situation . . . is simple," Lodge told a friend. "It has come down to Wilson's taking our reservations . . . or losing the treaty altogether." When the Democrats put pressure on Wilson he denounced the whole idea of reservations. There was no difference, he said, between "a nullifier" and "a mild nullifier."

Lodge, of course, did not have to make concessions. While he was not opposed in principle to joining the League, he did not believe that the League would ever be a success. If America did not join, he could dismiss the subject with a shrug. But Wilson's whole being was tied to the Covenant. His stubborn refusal to compromise was not based on reasoning. He was a man bereft of judgment, old, sick, self-deluded, and (the phrase is not too strong) incompetent to perform the duties of his office. The result was tragedy—personal, national, and world-wide. The Senate voted again in March, and came close to accepting the Treaty with the reservations. Half the Democrats (violating Wilson's express "orders") voted to ratify. The others, mostly Southern party hacks, joined with the irreconcilables, and together they mustered thirty-five votes, seven more than the one-third that meant defeat.

When Tumulty brought him word of the Senate's action, Wilson's only comment was: "They have shamed us in the eyes of the world."

What remains to be told is pitiful. Its theme is the crumbling of a once great intellect, the erosion of a forceful personality by age, disease, and disappointment. In April Wilson was able to meet with his Cabinet for the first time since his collapse, but, as one member noted, "it was enough to make one weep to look at him." The left side of his face drooped; his eyesight was so poor that the Department heads had to be introduced as they entered; he had difficulty concentrating on the subjects under discussion, and seemed unable to control the flow of thought from one topic to another. As a result, his administration stumbled through the last months of his term without plan or leadership. Strong men in the Cabinet ran their own Departments and plotted to win the succession. Weaker individuals let their Departments run themselves. Presidential messages, once so penetrating, became mere patchworks, drafted by bureaucrats and pinned together by Tumulty. The coming election colored everyone's thoughts.

Wilson did not realize the extent of his decline. He was determined that the election should be a "solemn referendum" on the League. What better plan than that he himself should captain the League forces? He was too weak, too befuddled to run a real campaign for a third nomination. Perhaps he never admitted to himself that he wanted it. But he would endorse no one else, nor would he withdraw his own name from consideration.

Loyal Joe Tumulty watched Wilson's maneuverings anxiously. No one knew better than he how impossible a third term would be, and how damaging to the chance of America's joining the League was Wilson's insistence on identifying himself with it. Already the Republicans were charging that he had defeated the reservations only to provide himself with an excuse for running again. Tumulty went into consultation with a crack reporter named Louis Siebold, who was eager to interview the President.

They prepared a list of loaded questions and answers.
Their purpose was to outline the issues on which the
coming election would be fought, and show that Wilson
was alert and *au courant* with public issues. But they also
intended to question him about his own plans, and draw
from him a renunciation of any desire for a third term.

Wilson would have none of this. He was glad to
grant the interview, but he would not answer many of
the questions. Mrs. Wilson told Tumulty that only material tending to glorify her husband should be published.
Tumulty's biographer, John M. Blum, records that the
secretary was so disgusted by her attitude that he wrote a
memorandum on her note of instructions "inviting her to
go to hell."

The interview took place, and received wide publicity. Wilson also permitted a photographer to snap him
signing papers vigorously at his desk. But the picture was
taken from the right, carefully concealing the ravaged
left side of his face. Instead of providing Wilson with a
graceful exit from the political scene, Tumulty's plan
served to create the impression that he was an active candidate for renomination.

But the hard-headed politicians who gathered at San
Francisco would not hear of him. When a deadlock developed and a fervent Wilson backer tried to push the
President forward, a group of them, including some of
the President's truest friends like Josephus Daniels and
Carter Glass, stifled the idea at its source. Postmaster General Burleson had the temerity to wire Wilson that William Gibbs McAdoo seemed likely to be nominated.
Wilson's only answer to this "disloyalty" was a telegram
to the chairman of the Democratic National Committee
suggesting that Burleson be excluded from further intimate conferences at San Francisco. It was only with the

greatest difficulty that he was later dissuaded from demanding Burleson's resignation.

The exasperating thing to the party leaders was that Wilson could have given the nomination to any of the leading candidates by a simple nod of his head. The politicians respected the President's right, as head of the party, to choose his successor. They were not disloyal—only practical. They knew he was no longer fit for the office. By his silence Wilson paralyzed the convention through forty-odd ballots, and opened wounds in the ranks that were slow in healing. Governor James M. Cox of Ohio finally won the nomination (with young Franklin D. Roosevelt as his running-mate), but much unnecessary damage had been done, purely because of Wilson's stubbornness and coyness.

Wilson was unable to take much part in the presidential campaign, and partially because of him his party was overwhelmed in the election. His obsession with the League, together with his illness, meant that his party had no coherent domestic program to offer the post-war world. The liberal coalition he had constructed fell apart for lack of leadership. His personal magic with the voters disappeared—no one likes a bitter, stubborn old man, and it was all too clear that this was what he had become. And while many Americans believed in the League, their number was dwindling under the assaults of the rampant nationalists. Few were ready to endorse Wilson's uncompromising stand for the Covenant without reservations.

Wilson was too much a fighter to be overwhelmed by defeat, but he was further depressed by it. He turned the routine task of preparing a Thanksgiving Proclamation over to a Cabinet member, because, he said, there did not seem to be much for him to be thankful for. His last months in the White House were passed in gloom. Mrs.

Wilson managed to distract him with plans for altering and redecorating their newly purchased residence on S Street, and he was cheered by news that he had been given the Nobel Peace Prize. He made a feeble attempt to resume a long-ago discarded study of the philosophy of politics, but of course such work was now beyond him. Chiefly, from November to March, he merely waited.

On inauguration day he donned his striped trousers and cutaway coat and rode with President-elect Harding to the Capitol. Wilson ignored the cheering crowds along the way, gazing straight ahead, his face haggard. At the Capitol he limped painfully along on his cane to the President's room in the Senate wing. There he occupied himself with the signing of last-minute bills. Members of his Cabinet were on hand, and one by one they came forward to shake his hand. General Pershing entered to pay his respects; other friends and associates joined the little group. Gradually Wilson mellowed, moved by the many expressions of good will.

Finally the last bill was signed. "Well," the President said cheerfully, "I think I had better scoot now." But as he prepared to rise, a group of congressmen filed into the room. It was a joint committee appointed to inform him that the work of the session was finished. Its spokesman was the Senate majority leader, Henry Cabot Lodge. Two old and bitter enemies faced each other for the last time. "This committee begs to inform you," said Lodge, "that the two Houses have completed their work and are prepared to receive any further communications from you."

Wilson flushed deeply. He glared at Lodge, his face set. "I have no further communication. I would be glad if you would inform both Houses and thank them for their courtesy. *Good morning, sir.*" Without another word he spun in his swivel chair, struggled to his feet, and hobbled from the room. A few minutes later Warren G. Harding took the oath of office. The Wilson era was over.

For three more years Wilson lived on, lonely and embittered. He was completely dependent upon his wife, who devoted her whole time to making him comfortable. She read so many detective stories to him that she found herself thinking in terms of crime. So they switched to Dickens and Scott. Sometimes old friends would drop in to chat, but talk was difficult. Wilson usually looked straight ahead, instead of at his interlocutor, and he spoke without animation. Only occasionally would the old fires burn again for a moment, as when one visitor mentioned Senator Lodge, or when Lord Robert Cecil discussed the work of the League of Nations. "We are winning!" Wilson assured Cecil. "Don't make any concessions!"

As he gradually declined, certain childlike qualities asserted themselves. His failing eyesight made close reading difficult, but he consumed picture magazines avidly: *Punch, House Beautiful*, eventually even the movie magazines. There was always a small table by his side, piled with such matter. He kept a magnifying glass and a flashlight at hand, which he used, according to Mrs. Wilson, to "study details" of the photographs. He took great pleasure in attending the vaudeville theater, where the slapstick comedians particularly delighted him. He also enjoyed the movies, and would beam with happiness at the applause that usually greeted his appearance on such occasions.

He remained officially silent on politics, but to the last he would not admit that his career was over. He was bitterly hostile to James M. Cox, and only less so to the men who had made Cox's 1920 nomination possible. He struggled spasmodically with the draft of a party platform (he called it "the Document") which was to revitalize the Democratic Party in 1924. Perhaps—he never denied it—he pictured Woodrow Wilson leading the Party back to power once again. Actually the Document was a sad affair; one historian has called it "an unimpressive repetition of old ideas." American membership in the League was its main plank.

It was typical of Wilson's frame of mind that he kept this platform a closely guarded secret, yet was resentful when Democratic leaders unknowingly expressed views contradictory to it. Wilson, for example, was very disturbed when Tumulty spoke against the Volstead Act, for the Document called for the strict enforcement of the Prohibition amendment. How poor Tumulty was to know this (Wilson, after all, had vetoed the Volstead Act) did not occur to him.

As late as December 1923 he still saw himself as the leader of world liberal opinion. To the suggestion of a well-meaning friend that he make his influence felt by running for the Senate, he replied: "There is only one place, you know, where I could be sure of effectively asserting . . . leadership." Besides, he added, "you know and I know that I have a temper, and if I was to go to the Senate, I would get in a row with that old Lodge, who no longer counts for anything. The Senate would hardly provide the place for liberal leadership that the world is seeking so sadly."

Fortunately, he was spared the final disillusionment that would surely have come to him in the 1924 campaign. Instead he died serene in his belief that he was still a great popular leader.

And in a sense, of course, he was. The passage of time

quickly dulled the edges of partisan hostility. More and more, although shorn of real influence, he began to exert an indirect influence upon his times. The ideals he had fought for retained their appeal, and as his powers waned, even his enemies came to appreciate his finer qualities— his faith in mankind, his fighting heart, his zeal for the public service, his personal courage in the face of his crippling infirmities.

On Armistice Day, 1923, a crowd gathered before the house on S Street. Wilson had spoken the evening before over the radio; now he was deluged with congratulatory messages. He responded with a brief speech from the front steps, a speech frequently interrupted by bursts of warm applause. He praised the soldiers who had won the war, and thanked his listeners for their kindness to him. Then, when the cheers had died down and he was about to retire, the spark within him flared once again:

Just one word more; I cannot refrain from saying it. I am not one of those who have the least anxiety about the triumph of the principles I have stood for. I have seen fools resist Providence before, and I have seen their destruction. . . . That we shall prevail is as sure as that God reigns. Thank you.

The door closed behind him to the accompaniment of a sustained ovation.

Six weeks later the end was at hand. On January 31 it became known that he was dying. For two days silent crowds stood reverently in S Street, and when, on the morning of February 3, he died, the faithful watchers bared their heads, and knelt in final tribute to his indomitable spirit.

Woodrow Wilson's place in history has been blurred

by the memory of his last great failure. Friend and foe have pounced upon it to justify his idealism or to flay his stubborn egotism. It is hardly fair to blame him for mistakes made when he was shattered in mind and body, but it is no more reasonable to insist that in his full health he would have saved the League and the world with it. Instead, posterity should judge him on his record before his collapse.

That he was a great man is beyond dispute. He had a first-rate mind, discerning, quick, and broad-gauged. He was a brilliant political leader and a high-minded statesman. His flaws were personal and beyond his control. No man ever needed the protection of human warmth and understanding more, but some inner insecurity drove him from his fellows. He lived too much within himself, drawing reassurance from absolutes—God, duty, justice. He set himself standards beyond human attainment, and, unable to admit his inevitable inadequacies, fled from his limitations into pitiable self-deception.

His life was full of achievement and honors. He ruled a great university, a great state, and a great nation. Vast crowds cheered his name. He dined with kings, and sat with the most powerful men of his age to remake the map of the world. His tragedy was that he never learned to live at peace with himself.

XII

IN one sense the life of a great man ends with his last heartbeat, in another it goes on as long as people retain an interest in his accomplishments. For a time after death he lives on in the memories of his contemporaries. But they too are mortal. In Wilson's case, for example, those who knew him well have already dwindled to an aging handful; in a decade or two none will be left.

The great man's permanent fame is dependent upon his biographers. The image he casts into the future is almost as much the product of their work as his own. Without their understanding and artistry, his reputation will meet a fate as final and disintegrating as the grave which holds his body; with their help it can endure forever.

> So long as men can breathe, or eyes can see,
> So long lives this, and this gives life to thee.

Thus Shakespeare boasted of his ability to grant a measure of immortality to his love. A biographer's sheer literary power can give an everlasting fame of sorts to the most unimportant subject. Few biographers possess such art, which is in the interests of justice, since it means that most men must make their own reputations. Yet if succeeding generations know Woodrow Wilson as his own did, it is in biographies that they make his acquaintance.

In this sense the life of a great man really *continues* after death, for it is not a static record that endures. His place in history is not fixed. He wins new triumphs, suffers further failures, as each generation judges him through the eyes of a succession of biographers. Therefore, an account of Wilson's life should not end without tracing his history from the grave to today.

Word-portraits of Wilson began to appear as soon as he achieved political prominence. The periodical literature between 1910 and 1924 is full of sketches and analyses of the man. There were also campaign biographies in 1912 and 1916. The most interesting of these early studies is William Bayard Hale's *Woodrow Wilson: The Story of His Life* (1912).

Hale was an Episcopal minister who turned to journalism. While he was on the staff of *World's Work*, editor Walter Hines Page arranged for him to write Wilson's biography. The book was well received, and Hale became friendly with the President-elect. It was he who edited Wilson's 1912 speeches, which were published as *The New Freedom*. In 1913 the President sent him as a special agent to Mexico, where his reports on conditions had a great deal to do with Wilson's refusal to recognize Huerta. But their friendship cooled, and Hale became associated with the pro-German faction in America after the outbreak of the war. He was in the direct pay of the German government, and when this fact was made public, he was disgraced. In 1920 he published *The Story of a Style*, a detailed analysis of Wilson's speeches designed to demonstrate the President's egotism and fuzziness of thought. The mass of evidence merits consideration, but the author's vindictiveness and his hatred of Wilson are so apparent that the objective reader must question his conclusions.

For the 1916 campaign Henry Jones Ford wrote *Woodrow Wilson: The Man and His Work*. Ford also had a newspaper background, but around the turn of the century he became interested in political problems and wrote a number of highly regarded treatises on government. Wilson brought him to Princeton in 1908 as Professor of Politics, appointed him to an administrative post

in the New Jersey government in 1912, and later sent
him to the Philippines on a mission similar to Hale's in
Mexico. When he wrote his campaign life, Ford was a
member of the Interstate Commerce Commission, a place
he held until the Harding regime took over in 1921.

In 1919 another journalist began to write a hasty
sketch about Wilson. He was Ray Stannard Baker,
writer for *McClure's* and the *American Magazine*. Baker
had a warm sympathy for the President, and had served
at the Versailles Conference as press-bureau director for
the American delegation. When Wilson undertook his
western tour, Baker produced a series of syndicated articles (later published in book form) entitled: *What Wilson Did At Paris*. The President was impressed, and after
he began to recover from his stroke, he persuaded Baker
to do a detailed study of the Conference, working from
Wilson's own collection of documents and papers. Baker
insisted on having a free hand, and Wilson readily agreed
to this. The three volumes, *Woodrow Wilson and World
Settlement*, appeared in 1922, and are still a major source
for that period of Wilson's career.

Without meaning to, Baker gradually came to make
Wilson his life work. After Wilson's death, he and Professor William E. Dodd of the University of Chicago undertook an edition of his public papers, published in six
volumes between 1925 and 1927. In 1925, Mrs. Wilson persuaded him to undertake a full-scale biography,
offering him access to her husband's vast collection of personal papers. He hesitated, since he had already devoted
several years to Wilson, but she carried the day by showing him a letter Wilson had written to him but never
sent, the last letter he ever wrote, in which he said:
"With regard to my personal correspondence and other
similar papers I shall regard you as my preferred credi-

tor. . . . I would rather have your interpretation of
them than that of anybody else I know. . . . Pray accept assurances of my unqualified confidence and affec-
tionate regard."

All of Baker's earlier work, being syndicated interna-
tionally, had sold very well, and it would have been easy
for him to have made a fortune by writing a brief and intimate life. One editor offered him a guarantee of two
hundred thousand dollars for such a piece. But once committed to the project, Baker determined to do a full-scale
job, free from the rush of deadlines. His *Woodrow Wilson, Life and Letters* appeared in eight volumes between
1927 and 1939, and is still the fullest treatment of most
of Wilson's career that we have. Baker approached his
task in the best possible spirit. "I *am* a friend of Wilson's," he admitted. "It is only by a friend that any man
can be understood. . . . "[But] merely to defend a
friend, thick or thin, is silly business, and raises him in the
estimation of no one. . . . My attitude is not one of defense but of explanation." Yet his biography is disappointing.

Baker lacked the scholarly training needed to handle
effectively the masses of source material at his disposal.
He acquired skill gradually as he worked, and his volumes on Wilson's first term are superior to the earlier
ones, but when he reached the war period he gave up.
The last two volumes deal with the years 1917 and 1918
in a purely chronological manner—they are no more
than source material. And despite twenty years of labor
and eighteen volumes, Baker never covered all of Wilson's life. His story ends with Wilson's return from Paris.
His books will always be useful, for he was a close ob-
server of much of the history he describes. He also provides copious extracts from documents and from Wilson's

letters, some of which have never been made available to other students. For an "authorized" biographer so closely identified with his subject, he is reasonably objective on most topics. But his work is not the definitive study he hoped to make it.

While Wilson lived, natural reticence dammed the flood of biographical sketches, but between 1924 and 1926 a number of lives were published. Books turned out in the years immediately after their subject's death are usually slick, empty, and eulogistic. Wilson, however, was fortunate in his early chroniclers. David Lawrence, a Washington correspondent, wrote *The True Story of Woodrow Wilson* in 1924. Lawrence was friendly but not uncritical; he drew upon personal knowledge of his subject and upon interviews. The result is first-rate—a book still useful and entertaining to read. Even better is James Kerney's *The Political Education of Woodrow Wilson* (1926). Kerney, of course, knew Wilson very well. His account of the gubernatorial years is detailed, candid, and full of insight. Thoroughly fair-minded from start to finish, his book is a basic source. Kerney admired Wilson and, unlike many early friends, remained on good terms with him throughout his life, but he was too honest, too deeply imbued with the newspaperman's healthy skepticism, and too intelligent, to write a gloss. As a biography *The Political Education* is unbalanced, with its heavy emphasis on 1910–12, but it is one of the finest of the character studies of Wilson. Kerney wrote of Wilson, with his journalist's gift for the pungent phrase: "He was not made for long honeymoons."

These are the best of the early lives. Others that should be mentioned are Professor Dodd's *Woodrow Wilson and His Work*, which, considering Dodd's scholarly background, is almost shamelessly partisan and eulogistic, and Robert E. Annin's *Woodrow Wilson*, a very unfriendly analysis by one who knew Wilson during the Princeton period. To Annin, Wilson was no more than an egotistical liar.

Along with these biographies came many memoirs written by persons associated with Wilson in one way or another. Some of these were published while he was still living. The wartime propaganda chief, George Creel, wrote *The War, the World, and Wilson* in 1920. This is a general defense of the administration's handling of the war and the peace. The next year William F. McCombs's *Making Woodrow Wilson President* presented a passionate description of the 1912 campaign, stressing Wilson's ingratitude to the author. Robert Lansing's impressions of the Versailles Conference, explaining his objections to the Treaty, his disagreements with Wilson, and his candid opinions of the chief Allied leaders, were given to the public in two volumes published in 1921: *The Big Four*, and *The Peace Negotiations, a Personal Narrative*.

The memoirs of Joseph P. Tumulty, *Woodrow Wilson as I Know Him*, one of the most important of this group, also came out in 1921. Tumulty's descriptions of conversations with Wilson are highly imaginative, and he displays a tendency to exaggerate his own importance, but his book contains many valuable documents and letters, and demonstrates his unswerving loyalty to his chief. Despite the laudatory tone of the book, it irritated Wilson, and its publication marked a big step in the deterioration of the Wilson-Tumulty friendship. In 1924 an edition of the *Letters* of Secretary of the Interior Franklin K. Lane, and the recollections of Secretary of Commerce Redfield, *With Congress and Cabinet*, were published, and in 1925 the *Memoirs of William Jennings*

Bryan, and the *Recollections of Thomas R. Marshall,* Wilson's Vice-President, added their bulk to the growing mass. Secretary of Agriculture David F. Houston published *Eight Years with Wilson's Cabinet* in 1926. This is a careful and intelligent commentary on the administration and includes a sympathetic yet objective portrait of the President.

Colonel House's vitally important impressions of the Wilson years appeared in four volumes published in 1926 and 1928. *The Intimate Papers of Colonel House,* ably edited by Charles Seymour, contains copious extracts from the House diaries, and many letters from House to Wilson. The editor was unfortunately not permitted to publish Wilson's side of the correspondence, but he describes Wilson's reactions to House as fully as possible. *The Intimate Papers* remains one of the most important printed sources on Wilson's career as President.

In the thirties there were few attempts to write Wilson's life. Perhaps biographers shied away from the subject because of the Baker volumes, which came out sporadically through the decade. But the memoirs continued to pour forth. In 1930 Bainbridge Colby, who had replaced Lansing as Secretary of State in 1920, wrote *The Close of Woodrow Wilson's Administration and the Final Years.* Colby had been on excellent terms with Wilson, "representing" him at the 1920 convention. After Wilson retired, he and Colby formed a law partnership, which was soon dissolved because of Wilson's scrupulous refusal to accept business that might be influenced by his past connection with the government. Colby's brief account of this period of Wilson's life is less than candid, but contains information not available elsewhere. William Gibbs McAdoo's *Crowded Years* (1931) is less rewarding than one might expect, considering that Mc-

Adoo was an "original Wilson man" and the President's
son-in-law.

A third volume of Lansing recollections, the Secretary's *War Memoirs*, published in 1935, contains some
useful material. Wilson's daughter, Eleanor McAdoo,
also added valuable evidence in 1937, when her *The
Woodrow Wilsons* came out. Edith Bolling Wilson's
My Memoir (1939) is one of the most important remi-
niscences of Wilson. While her story is partisan, it is full
of intimate details, and unrivaled in its account of the President's illness and last years. Although it is an attempt to
justify Mrs. Wilson's actions while her husband was in-
capacitated, it is actually the clearest proof available that
he should have resigned in October 1919. Mrs. Wilson's
unfriendly estimate of Colonel House, while exaggerated, is quite shrewd.

After the outbreak of World War II, the growing
threat of American involvement greatly stimulated interest in Wilson. In 1941 David Loth, a skillful popular
biographer, published *Woodrow Wilson: The Fifteenth
Point*. He wrote "to help interpret for today the lesson
we failed to learn yesterday," and he places great stress
on Wilson's individual role in the events of 1914–20.
The "fifteenth point" is Wilson's personality, and Loth's
general view of his subject is sympathetic. His book was
the first to make full use of Baker's work and of the ex-
tensive memoir material that had come out.

Loth's book preceded Pearl Harbor. After the United
States entered the war the emphasis in Wilson research
shifted to the League of Nations period, for there was a
widespread realization that much could be learned about
peacemaking from an analysis of Wilson's actions during
and after World War I. Of these studies the most important are Thomas A. Bailey's *Woodrow Wilson and*

the Lost Peace (1944), and his *Woodrow Wilson and the Great Betrayal* (1945). While not true biographies, Bailey's books provide an excellent analysis of Wilson's role at Versailles and after. Adding an exhaustive study of the papers of Wilson and of his contemporaries to the available printed sources, Professor Bailey produced the first really fair-minded and dispassionate treatment of this most controversial period of Wilson's life. He stresses Wilson's essential good will, and the many positive achievements at Paris, and he points up the difficulties that made perfection impossible. But at the same time he emphasizes the extent to which Wilson's vague idealism encouraged hopes impossible of consummation, and he stresses the effect of the President's tactical errors. In the end he places the blame for defeat of the Treaty chiefly on Wilson, though again his careful analysis shows that the President's ill-health made it impossible for him to judge the situation accurately.

Shortly after Bailey's second volume came out, H. C. F. Bell's *Woodrow Wilson and the People* was published. Bell's interpretation, full of warmth and understanding, is marred only by his apologetic handling of the League question. His treatment of Wilson's personality is most convincing, particularly his explanation of his subject's complex attitude toward his friends. But writing at a time when international co-operation was foremost in men's minds, Bell glossed over Wilson's mistakes in 1919–1920 in order to emphasize his admittedly brilliant understanding of the futility of isolationism and the importance of a just peace.

This period also produced some interesting new memoirs. Margaret Randolph Elliott, a cousin of Wilson's, wrote *My Aunt Louisa and Woodrow Wilson* in 1944, offering many useful glimpses of his family life. Josephus

Daniels's *The Wilson Era* (1944, 1946) presents a hodge-podge of material of varying importance and reliability, drawn from his recollections as Secretary of the Navy. Daniels must be read with great caution, particularly when he quotes from his so-called diary. Actually his "diary" consists only of scattered notes and cryptic memoranda, which he expanded and embroidered in his volumes. At one point, for example, he quotes himself as wishing (in 1917!) that the public could have seen Wilson on television.

Of greater importance are two books of recollections by former Princeton colleagues of Wilson. Winthrop M. Daniel's privately printed *Recollections of Woodrow Wilson* (1944) is very brief, but *Woodrow Wilson, Some Princeton Memories* (1946), edited by William Starr Myers, contains a number of shrewd estimates by professors who were Wilson's contemporaries at the University.

Unfortunately, none of these books, nor even all of them collectively, is a definitive biography of Woodrow Wilson. Thirty-odd years of research and recollection leave the story still incomplete. But there is evidence that this will not be so for long. Since the late thirties Arthur S. Link of Northwestern University has been working on a massive study of every aspect of Wilson's life. Only one volume has appeared so far, *Wilson, the Road to the White House* (1947), but others are promised shortly. Eventually Professor Link plans eight volumes, after which there will be little still to be learned about Wilson's career.

But though all the facts may become known, the meaning of the facts will always remain debatable. Link approached his subject with reverence, attracted by the idealism of Wilson's public speeches. Yet his study of the records led him to some devastating criticisms. In *Wilson, the Road to the White House,* and in *Woodrow Wilson and the Progressive Era* (which is not part of the biography) he pictures Wilson as stubborn, vain, frequently hypocritical, and far less liberal than the superficial study of his career would indicate. But while Link's researches may make unnecessary further detailed study of the facts of Wilson's life, the meaning of these facts will remain debatable so long as Wilson's life retains any significance for Americans.

A great man's reputation tends to fluctuate with the passage of time, for each generation views him from a different perspective. Wilson's has suffered in recent years as our experiences with another world settlement have pointed up the flaws in his oversimplified approach to the problems of peace and war, just as it soared high in the disillusioned twenties when people admired him for his effort to "keep us out of war," and higher still in the early forties, when his vision of permanent peace based on a league of all the nations seemed about to be realized. But the true test of greatness is lasting interest in the man and his deeds. Woodrow Wilson's struggle with his life and his times still interests a world which continues to bear the imprint of his actions and his enigmatic personality. All signs indicate that this interest will not soon flag, and thus the parade of Wilson biographies will go on.

INDEX